Speaking Faithfully

Speaking Faithfully

Communications as Evangelism in a Noisy World

JIM NAUGHTON & REBECCA WILSON

Morehouse Publishing
NEW YORK · HARRISBURG · DENVER

Unless otherwise noted, the Scripture quotations contained herein are from the New Revised Standard Version Bible, copyright © 1989 by the Division of Christian Education of the National Council of Churches of Christ in the U.S.A. Used by permission. All rights reserved.

Morehouse Publishing, 4775 Linglestown Road, Harrisburg, PA 17112
Morehouse Publishing, 445 Fifth Avenue, New York, NY 10016
Morehouse Publishing is an imprint of Church Publishing Incorporated.
www.churchpublishing.org

Cover design by Laurie Klein Westhafer
Typeset by Vicki K. Black

Library of Congress Cataloging-in-Publication Data
Naughton, Jim.
  Speaking faithfully : communications as evangelism in a noisy world /
Jim Naughton and Rebecca Wilson.
      p.   cm.
  Includes bibliographical references.
  ISBN 978-0-8192-2810-9 (pbk.) — ISBN 978-0-8192-2811-6 (ebook)
  1. Oral communication—Religious aspects–Christianity. 2. Preaching.
  3. Evangelistic work. I. Wilson, Rebecca Webb. II. Title.
BV4597.53.C64N38 2012
269'.2—dc23

2012029847

Printed in the United States of America

For Jim's parents,
Frank and Alice Naughton,
who show him what it means to live a life of faith.

In memory of Rebecca's grandmother,
Mary Jeroline Councill Gladstone.

Contents

Acknowledgments

This book exists only because of the work we have been privileged to do for our clients.

Jim's first experience in church communications came in working with Bishop John Bryson Chane in the Diocese of Washington and Rebecca's came in working with Dean Tracey Lind at Trinity Cathedral in Cleveland. We are grateful to them both for the opportunities they provided and the confidence they extended.

We have learned volumes about spiritual leadership and grace under pressure from Bishops Jeffrey Lee, Mark Beckwith, and Mariann Budde.

The people of the Chicago Consultation have led some of the most important work we have ever done, and their spirit exemplifies the church speaking faithfully. Special thanks to Jen Adams, Brian Baker, Fredrica Harris Thompsett, Ruth Frey, Lowell Grisham, Gary Hall, Harry Knox, Ernesto Medina, Ruth Meyers, and especially Bonnie Perry.

Bishop Sean Rowe is morally courageous, astonishingly smart, and a good friend. His encouragement, advice, and preaching help sustain us.

Gay Clark Jennings is a dear friend, counselor, and client, and both our business and our souls owe much to her kindness. Her wit and good humor have sustained us through dull days and dark moments and taught us to take the gospel more seriously than we take ourselves.

Bishop Gene Robinson gave us his time and advice generously when we were beginning our business venture. He is a master of communications as evangelism and we continue to learn from his bravery and good humor.

Many other friends and clients have made it possible for us to learn and practice what we have written about in this book. Thanks especially to Bonnie Anderson, Jennifer Baskerville-Burrows, Robert Bottoms, Paul Cooney, Marianne Duddy-Burke and the people of Equally Blessed, Miguel Escobar, Lane Hensley, Elizabeth Jameson, Bill Joseph, Rebecca McDonald, Carly Rowe, and the people of the Dioceses of Chicago, Northern Michigan, Northwestern Pennsylvania, and Washington. The people of the reorganizing dioceses of Fort Worth, Pittsburgh, Quincy, and San Joaquin have taught us and the entire Episcopal Church about persevering in faith.

As Canticle has grown, we have had the astonishingly good fortune to work with Ellie Rencher, without whose organization, skill, and grace we would be utterly lost, and Lu Stanton Leon, whose skills as a journalist are outmatched only by her boundless enthusiasm. We have fun at work because we work with Ellie and Lu.

We were grateful—and fortunate—to have had the ever-patient and always insightful Stephanie Spellers as our editor, Mary Wilson as our first reader, and Vicki K. Black as our copy editor.

Rebecca would like to thank Nancy Bryan, Jim Simon, Ruth Frey, and Kristen Neuschel for keeping her headed in the right direction. Her son, Jacob, ate many hastily prepared dinners during the writing of this book and only rolled his eyes a few times when his mother took her laptop to his baseball games.

Jim would like to thank the blogging team at Episcopal Café, especially John Chilton, Ann Fontaine, Andrew Gerns, and Bishop Nicholas Knisely, who have labored longest; the Café's readers; his parents, Frank and Alice Naughton; Monsignor Joseph Kelly; Mary Sulerud; and his sons, Ben and Chris, who inspire and sustain him.

Introduction

A "Robust Baptismal Ecclesiology"?

A few years ago, we were working with an advocacy group eager to prevail in a hotly contested vote in their church's next legislative session. The issue at stake had attracted the attention of the mainstream media, and we were helping the group develop a few of the points that they hoped to make in conversations with reporters. What do you need to say, we asked them, to persuade people who do not currently agree with your position to consider changing their minds? How can you best articulate that message in an interview with a reporter from, say the Associated Press or *The New York Times*?

We threw these questions open for debate, and the group converged on a single answer quickly. The conversation went something like this:

"We will tell them that we have a robust baptismal ecclesiology."

"A robust baptismal ecclesiology?"

"Yes, a robust baptismal ecclesiology."

As it happens, we are church geeks, and can offer a passable explanation of what it means to be motivated by a baptismal ecclesiology, robust or otherwise. But church geeks are thin on the ground, and religion reporters know this. There was no chance that a reporter would quote this language, and every chance that said reporter would identify our clients as the kind of people who spoke in coded academic language and were therefore a waste of reportorial time.

Worse, there was little chance that people in the church's assembly who felt themselves stumbling toward a personal resolution of their own conflicted feelings about a vigorously contested issue were going to respond favorably to an argument couched in language they might not easily understand.

We asked the group to explain in language accessible to the average reader of an American newspaper what they meant by a robust baptismal ecclesiology, and began to copy some of the key phrases to use in crafting some simple declarative sentences. During this exercise, Rebecca said she understood the desire to speak in the language of one's specialty, but that during the upcoming legislative gathering those who felt tempted to use the phrase "robust baptismal ecclesiology" should find someone with as many or more advanced theological degrees as they had themselves and chat away—in a corner where no one else could hear.

In the end, the group developed a resonant set of messages, used them extremely effectively, worked in coalition with other likeminded people, and passed the legislation in question. Success, as the saying goes, has many parents, and our clients may well have prevailed had they spoken in the jargon of their field, or not spoken at all. But we take it as a bedrock principle that if you are going to speak, you should make the effort required to speak effectively. You owe it to yourself, your cause, and, not least, to your audience.

Insider Conversations

The church, particularly the mainline Protestant churches, has trouble speaking effectively. We have the "robust baptismal ecclesiology" problem. That is, we say things that other people do not understand, and are surprised when they do not respond in the ways we had hoped. (Perhaps you know someone who has instructed newcomers to meet him in the narthex after the doxology to discuss their catechesis, and then wondered why no one showed up.)

The use of specialized language is symptomatic of a larger problem. Often, when we speak, we speak primarily to ourselves. Visit a random selection of mainline parish websites and ask yourself if the site helps those seeking a new church home to make an intelligent decision about whether it would be worthwhile to spend a Sunday morning in this parish. Many church websites are aimed almost exclusively at the people who already participate in the community. (And perhaps, in an unfortunate and unintended way, that *does* give seekers the information they need about exploring the parish in question.)

When we speak to the outside world through the media, social media, or advertising, we are frequently informing the populace that we in the mainline churches are doing what we have always done for those who are still interested in our doing it. A friend in the media relations business said he had lost count of the times he had been asked to drum up interest for a story that boiled down to "priest preaches in church on Sunday." To be clear, we often benefit from listening to clergy preach in church, but the practice is well established, and the vast swath of humankind that didn't show up last week probably isn't going to show up because you have informed them that you are doing it again this week.

> We may speak to ourselves because we have lost confidence in our ability to speak to others.

Some of the less charitable analysts of the mainline churches have suggested we speak primarily to ourselves because we are self-obsessed. Perhaps. But we may also speak to ourselves because we have lost confidence in our ability to speak to others. Mainline Protestants have a tendency to describe themselves in terms of what they are not. They are not Roman Catholics, perhaps because they object to that church's positions on women's ordination, or the morality of same-sex relationships, or to the monarchical character of the papacy. They are not members of the religious right, with whom they may differ on issues from the authority of scripture to the political issues of the moment. Mainline Protestants are, in many ways, the Christians most at home in contemporary culture, and while that may distinguish us from other Christians, it does not distinguish us from the majority of other people. So who are we?

Our ability to answer this question in a useful way is hampered by what, in many ways, is a virtue. We don't like to offend people—at least not gratuitously. We believe there should be a place for everyone in our communities. Hence the frequent use of the words "inclusive" and "diverse" in our literature. While our denominational leaders and legislatures often take progressive political positions, on the parish level most of our communities are more at home doing hands-on works of mercy than organizing and advocating for justice. Mainline Protestants tend to be swing voters, and while some denominations are more liberal than others, on the parish level, where we have to get along on a week-by-week basis, we are driven by a desire to focus on matters that unite rather than divide. There is a certain wisdom in this, but it can make it more difficult to articulate precisely what one's congregation stands for beyond a willingness to treat the views of current members with respect.

A Voice Is a Terrible Thing to Waste

In our work, we attempt to help faith communities to identify their distinctive gifts and their most treasured values, and then to speak about these matters to the particular audiences that God has put in front of them. Although it may sound strange given the declining vitality of mainline denominations, this enterprise is not always considered to be valuable. In a number of communities and denominations, communications positions and budgets are the first to be cut when fiscal times get tight. Additionally, church leaders, who may be decent communicators themselves, often assume that they know as much as they need to know about the field—an attitude that it is difficult to imagine them holding about, say, the law, or accounting. Conversely, they may think of communications primarily as a matter of maintaining the proper technologies, acknowledge that they are out of their depth in this area, and entrust the entire endeavor to an information technology specialist.

> It is not enough to live faithfully. We must speak faithfully, as well.

Finally, there is a frequently expressed bit of half-formed wisdom that the church simply needs to live out the gospel in order to attract people to Christ. We suspect, however, that it is not enough to live faithfully. We must speak faithfully, as well. We must proclaim our faith, as well as embody it. And to tell our story to contemporary audiences, we must baptize the tools and techniques that other organizations use to spread their message, inform their members, influence society, raise money, and engender the devotion and enthusiasm necessary to sustain their communities.

Who Are You People?

We come at this task from rather different but (we'd like to think) mutually reinforcing perspectives.

Jim likes to say that he followed the well-worn path from covering Major League Baseball to working in the Episcopal Church. A former journalist, he has worked at *The New York Times, The Daily News* (where he covered the New York Mets, hence the baseball reference), and *The Washington Post,* among other places. He also helped to launch Beliefnet.com before spending seven years as the canon for communications in the Episcopal Diocese of Washington.

He is a former Roman Catholic who joined the Episcopal Church in his early forties. He had some formative spiritual experiences while working and traveling in El Salvador and South Africa, and has been deeply influenced by the Catholic social justice tradition, the writings of St. John of the Cross, and the Episcopal Church's understanding that lay people share authority and responsibility in governing the church. He has, as you may have guessed, a robust baptismal ecclesiology.

Rebecca came to work in the church after more than a decade of communications and grant-seeking for nonprofit and public sector organizations. She helped pass non-partisan ballot issues that supported public libraries, urban public schools, and mental health treatment, among other good causes, and spent years advocating for children in Ohio, a state where politics will break your heart.

By accident of a mixed marriage between an Episcopalian and a Presbyterian, she grew up as a fish-out-of-Calvinist-water, except on visits to her maternal grandmother. But Nana's influence was stronger even than predestination, and she found her way back to the Episcopal Church in her early thirties after the obligatory young adult decade away from organized religion. She believes in the Baptismal Covenant, the Easter Vigil, and her inalienable right to keep her theology to herself.

In 2009, Jim was serving on the steering committee of the Chicago Consultation, an advocacy organization in the Episcopal Church, and planning to handle their communications at the church's upcoming General Convention. Then the president of the church's House of Deputies asked him to handle her communications as well. Knowing he couldn't handle both jobs, he contacted Rebecca, whom he had met just once at a conference and knew primarily from conversations on a listserv. Rebecca agreed to work with the Chicago Consultation and to contribute stories about General Convention to Episcopal Café, the church news website that Jim and a team of volunteers had created in 2007.

If you have been through the intensive legislative and social whirlwind that is the General Convention (or, we suspect, any other denominational legislative gathering), you know that if you can work closely with someone through those long and often tense days without getting sick of him or her, it is a testament to your tolerance for one another. Jim, who had been considering leaving his job before his bishop announced his retirement, finished most of the year working for the diocese, and he and Rebecca formed Canticle Communications in December 2009. A canticle, as you may know, is a song of praise.

Working together, we have developed a shared understanding of what it means to speak faithfully using the tools available to contemporary communicators. We believe that it is essential to develop an understanding of your community's gifts and priorities; to distill this understanding into a few easily understood message points; to use those message points to help you tell stories that demonstrate what God is doing in the lives of your people and your community; to tell those stories in text, sound, images, and moving images; to tell them in a way that will appeal to the audiences you are trying to reach; and to distribute these stories through traditional media and social networks.

> In our reluctance to sound like televangelists, the mainline churches sometimes sound like a well-intentioned service organization, or a political movement, or a social club for the terminally inoffensive.

We believe it is essential, in telling these stories, not to force a message on people, but to keep the example of those whose stories you tell in the forefront. At the same time, it is important not to focus so tightly on the work of the church that you neglect to mention the faith that inspires it. In our understandable reluctance to sound like the more egregious televangelists, the mainline churches sometimes sound like a well-intentioned service organization, or a political movement, or a social club for the terminally inoffensive. But if that is all the church has to offer, it has no unique reason for existing.

Our role as communicators is to make our neighbors say: "Something is happening with those people that I want to know more about." Or even, "Something is happening with these people that I want to be part of." Our job is to pique interest, to catalyze exploration, to issue invitations. To put it in more reductive terms, our task is to help instill the desire that gets someone through your door the first time, and then to provide the information and inspiration that keeps them there.

We are about the business of cultivating relationships with people who may not even know they are seeking a relationship.

What follows are some of our thoughts on how that can best be done. We'd like to think those thoughts will be helpful to professional church communications people interested in broadening their skills or taking a more strategic approach to their work, folks with solid communications backgrounds who have not previously worked in the church, and volunteers looking for a way to jump-start their ministry. We know that in many parishes and some judicatories, bishops, clergy, or staff members with little knowledge of contemporary communications are forced to develop a budget for a communications ministry, supervise its execution, and perhaps even execute it themselves. We hope this book will allow them to feel confident, and maybe even just a little bit bold.

CHAPTER 1

The Theological Imperative

Following Jesus

Jesus, as you may be aware, was something of a storyteller, and he went to significant lengths to make himself heard. If you doubt this, try giving a sermon while standing in an open boat.

Jesus was more than just a good storyteller, of course. But not less. He had something urgent and enormously important to say, and he said it in an extremely creative way.

To use the jargon of our field for a moment, Jesus had a very definite message: The kingdom of God is at hand. He unfolded it in ever-greater depth, and developed a network of sympathetic people who could carry his message beyond the reach of his own voice. He explained complex theological truths in language that fishermen, tax collectors, and women who lived on the margins of society could understand. He understood his diverse audiences extremely well, and knew how to argue scripture and law with Pharisees and how to tell earthy parables that caught the imagination of less educated audiences. He told tales that were vivid, memorable, and open to deeper exploration. We knew a Christian education director once who said that the resurrection was all well and good, but she would have believed that Jesus was the Son of God simply because he had come up with the parable of the prodigal son.

As familiar as the teachings and stories of Jesus are, it can be helpful to people involved in communications to stop and consider them strictly in terms of literary achievement. There are thirty-five distinct parables, give or take, depending on which scholars are doing the counting. That's a lot of writing. We do not see Jesus scribbling anything down (perhaps because that would be anachronistic) or rehearsing his delivery so that he can hear how the words he had heard only in his mind sounded on his lips. But make no mistake; stories as sophisticated as the Good Samaritan seldom blossom fully formed in an author's head.

> Jesus knew how to use the characters, landscape, and situations of his stories to let his audience know that he knew their world, their hopes, their failings, and their fears.

A storyteller who can convey the tenderness at the heart of the parable of the lost sheep, plumb the depths of human selfishness in the tale of Lazarus and the rich man, define the kingdom of God by speaking about seeds and birds and bushes, and cook up a parable just about every time he passes a fig tree is practicing his craft at an exalted level. Perhaps all of this came easily, Jesus being who he was. Perhaps not. The point isn't so much that Jesus worked hard at this—though we suspect that he did—but that he understood the importance of speaking in fresh and inventive ways. He knew how to use the characters, landscape, and situations of his stories to let his audience know that he knew their world, their hopes, their failings, and their fears.

Jesus' life was even more captivating than his teachings. He lived in a way that riveted attention, and reinforced the revelation that he preached. There was no discrepancy between what he said and what he did. That kind of authenticity confers credibility, which is essential when you are inviting people to make significant changes in their lives. Obviously Jesus performed certain feats that are beyond any church communications person we have encountered, but telling compelling stories, and living in ways that suggest we take those stories seriously, are not among them.

The Apostle Paul:
All Things to All Audiences

St. Paul's example hits even closer to home for the contemporary communicator. He knew seemingly every port of call in the Mediterranean and preached to much more diverse audiences than those that followed Jesus. As a well-educated Jew, a Roman citizen, and a Christian theologian, he was able to speak in ways that could be understood by people of different religious, cultural, and ethnic backgrounds.

Paul was well aware of the advantage this gave him. In 1 Corinthians 9:20–22 he wrote: "To the Jews I became as a Jew, in order to win Jews. To those under the law I became as one under the law...so that I might win those under the law. To those outside the law I became as one outside the law...so that I might win those outside the law. To the weak I became weak, so that I might win the weak. *I have become all things to all people, that I might by all means save some."*

One writer has suggested that Paul's extensive, cross-cultural missionary travels and his willingness to take on the mindset of his various audiences in order to win them over made him the first Christian target marketer. We raise that notion without fully endorsing it, to make it clear that even as single-minded an evangelist as Paul understood that he could not effectively communicate with all of the members of his culturally disparate audience at the same time.

Study his missionary travels, and you encounter a man who knew where and when he was most likely to receive a favorable hearing. He sought Jews in the synagogue and Greeks in the marketplace. He spent much of his time in cities, yet he didn't simply target the biggest population center in his path. The language of his letters is often dense, clause laden, and highly qualified, suggesting it was honed in debate. But few passages ever captured on paper are more graceful and grace-filled than the beginning of the thirteenth chapter of his first letter to the Corinthians, where he writes, "Love is patient; love is kind; love is not envious or boastful or arrogant or rude. . . . It bears all things, believes all things, hopes all things, endures all things" (1 Corinthians 13:4, 7).

Some scholars have looked for a particular strategy in Paul's travels, but there isn't one strategy—there are many. And like modern communicators who are called upon to use new tools before they have mastered them, Paul is always adapting, finding his way, shifting his plans whether due to shipwreck or some new opportunity. And all to tell a story that changes lives, including his own life.

The Hyenas Did Not Touch Him

It is worth remembering the practices of Jesus and Paul because those of us who attempt to spread the good news today often encounter resistance—not just from secular audiences, which is to be expected, but also from church leaders who labor under the false impression that mastering the use of the tools of the communications industry and the wisdom of public relations is somehow beneath the church. These leaders seem to believe the church should grow simply because it has opened its doors and continues to conduct its well-meaning business on Sunday mornings.

Despite the examples of Jesus and Paul, or, for that matter John Wesley, Billy Sunday, or Bishop Fulton J. Sheen, the church has been agonizingly slow to realize that communications is a ministry in its own right, not simply a support for "real" ministry. When parishes, dioceses, and churches are economizing, they will often cut communications budgets first. Parishes that would never dream of having a volunteer organist are happy to turn their communications ministry over to volunteers with no background in communications, and no opportunity to receive training.

Any number of church leaders will tell you that they did not establish an online presence because they were too busy building the church or feeding the hungry or visiting the sick—as though somehow learning to speak about these things in a way that gets others involved detracts from and is less sacred than these activities. But it is not a small thing to be able to put the word of God and the activities of God's people in front of people. The printing press helped make the Reformation possible. The radio supported the growth of the vast network of nondenominational megachurches across the country. We probably don't need to tell you that certain evangelists have built careers and fortunes from broadcasting their sermons on television.

> The church has been agonizingly slow to realize that communications is a ministry in its own right, not simply a support for "real" ministry.

People have always been eager to tell the story of God in their own times. We see this in the ways that the image of Jesus has been placed in settings and cultures across two millennia—note how Italian Renaissance paintings set the nativity in the palaces of burghers—and in the ways prayers are written to express timeless truths to people far removed from first-century Palestine and possibly unversed in the traditions of the Western Church.

Back in the sixteenth century, having the Bible in your own language was thought to be such a dangerous thing that Thomas More wanted to kill William Tyndale for making it possible. Having the liturgy in one's own language was a cause of great celebration for Roman Catholics after the Second Vatican Council. It is easy for us to appreciate when the word of God is made accessible to a culture we consider exotic. Think of the words of the Maasai Creed:

> We believe that God made good his promise by sending his son, Jesus Christ, a man in the flesh, a Jew by tribe, born poor in a little village, who left his home and was always on safari doing good, curing people by the power of God, teaching about God and man, showing that the meaning of religion is love. He was rejected by his people, tortured and nailed hands and feet to a cross, and died. He lay buried in the grave, *but the hyenas did not touch him,* and on the third day, he rose from the grave. He ascended to the skies. He is the Lord.

We can see that this is poetry, and that it is a skillful and devout attempt to reach new audiences and to articulate the distinctive way they understand the Christian faith. We understand the necessity of expressing Christianity in a way that speaks to the Maasai, but too often we do not grasp the importance of expressing Christianity in a way that speaks to twenty-first-century Americans.

Waiting for the Fish to Jump In

When we're speaking to groups, Jim sometimes asks people how they like his shoes, knowing full well that most of the people in the room cannot see them. You are not likely to buy a pair of shoes you can't see on the say-so of the salesman. Similarly, you are not likely to form a relationship with a church that provides you with little information about itself. Jesus said that no one lights a lamp and puts it under a bushel basket (Matthew 5:15), but Jesus had never met any Episcopalians or other mainline Christians. As a rule, we have been reluctant to call attention to ourselves. We are more comfortable being the church invisible, the church inoffensive, the church optional, and the church afraid of being associated with intolerant and heavy-handed people who are also Christian.

We need to get over this, but we won't do that by illuminating the interiors of bushel baskets. We won't do it by speaking in inoffensive generalities about kindness and politeness. Nor will we do it by announcing that we're having a potluck supper.

Rather, what is required of us are compelling accounts of what our faith means to us, clear explanations of the nature of our spiritual experiences, descriptions of our church communities as places where people are committed to working for justice and peace, and stories about the ways that God has changed our lives and the lives of people we know. These can be hard stories to tell, and hard institutional communications to produce for people who sometimes hold inoffensiveness as a high virtue. But it is possible that the future of our churches depend upon it.

Even the word "evangelism" makes some people feel uncomfortable. We have worked with church communicators who argued hard and successfully against our efforts to include information about what Episcopalians believe and how they worship on their website. They were happy to have it conveyed on parish sites, or on the website of the Episcopal Church. They just didn't want it on their site. We think this is symptomatic of the fear and unease that what people sometimes refer to as the "E word" arouses.

> The Episcopal Church's approach to evangelism is similar to setting an aquarium on the shore of the ocean and waiting for fish to jump in.

The Most Reverend Frank Griswold, former presiding bishop of the Episcopal Church, once said that the Episcopal Church's approach to evangelism was similar to setting an aquarium on the shore of the ocean and waiting for fish to jump in. That doesn't work in an age in which churchgoing is no longer socially normative. We live increasingly in an on-demand world where activities that once required us to be in a specific place at a specific time (television shows, movies) can be indulged on our own schedule. We live in a culture in which youth soccer and other sports compete for the affection of our children, and there is no longer a taboo against holding those activities on Sunday mornings. Fear-based motivations for attending church (to avoid going to hell or being seen as an outcast by one's neighbors) have lost their force, and people who think of themselves as "spiritual but not religious" look to Oprah as a spiritual guide, to therapists for moral direction, and to book clubs and cycling groups for their sense of community.

Churches are up against all of those competing forces. Too often we respond by retreating to the comfortable place in which we communicate primarily, even exclusively, with our own members. Take a look at a few church websites. Which ones seem more like they belong on an *intra*net than on the *Inter*net? How many take a "member services" approach to communications aimed at making it convenient for those already in the church to find the information they need quickly and then be on their way? This doesn't make much sense as a web strategy. Your highly motivated regular visitors are already deeply familiar with your site. They do not need primary homepage real estate to draw them into the church, and after a visit or two they are going to know how to find what they need. Instead, the homepage of a church website is for the stranger who needs the real welcome, and who wants a deeper understanding of what the church is about.

We have not yet awakened from the dream of a time when aspiring to mainline Protestantism was part of rising into the middle class, and coffee hour was an extension of Saturday night at the club or Sunday afternoon on the golf course. We have not yet adjusted to the fact that the world, in many places, has passed us by, or that to catch up we have to tell a story that shows we have been meeting God and living lives of genuine faith all the while.

So, let us go on a safari to lift some bushels and light some lights. With any luck, the hyenas will not touch us.

CHAPTER 2

Aaron Sorkin Goes to Church

Naughty Words in Church

There are words that don't go down especially well in church contexts, that make people worry that you are going to shift into Aaron Sorkin's *West Wing* mode and force them to engage in witty, rapid fire banter as they walk quickly from one important meeting to the next. "Messaging" is one of those words.

To many listeners, the word "messaging" speaks of either marketing or electioneering. It connotes a lack of authenticity and an effort to frame truth in a way that obscures truth. We would like to propose a different definition. A message is the thing you want to say. Messaging is the process you participate in to figure out your message.

Let's try another naughty word: "audience." Or, to make things a little more risqué, "target audience." Because the church wants to speak to as wide an audience as possible—to "go therefore and make disciples of all nations" (Matthew 28:19)—church folks resist the notion that their audience is anything less than humankind. They imagine it is sinful to be anything less than entirely inclusive. We think this constitutes a misunderstanding of our role as individual Christians or members of a particular community. Just as none of us sees the whole truth, none of us has the appeal necessary to speak to "everyone." And yet, many congregations and not a few dioceses define their target audience just that way.

Each individual and each congregation has particular gifts, opportunities, and responsibilities to speak to particular audiences. Some of these audiences are given to us because our community has demonstrated a certain ability to attract them, others because they live in our neighborhoods. But however God gives them to us, they are ours, and we need to learn how to say what we have to say in a way that they will find compelling.

In this chapter, we're going to delve into messaging and audience targeting church-style, not Washington Beltway-style. But it won't hurt you to fire up those *West Wing* reruns to get in the mood.

The Tragedy of the Trifold Brochure

We once knew a parish whose leaders enthusiastically told us that they needed a trifold brochure. There was a college nearby, and their plan was to induce the college students to come to their 9:00 a.m. contemporary music service and hand them a brochure with an information card inserted. The college students, they explained, would then fill out the cards with their contact information and the church would send them a welcome packet via the U.S. mail.

It's fun to hunt for as many examples of institutional church myopia as you can find in this little vignette, but for communications purposes, the point is this: If you skip the work of developing the messages that will most effectively reach your key audiences and identifying those audiences carefully, you risk having a communications plan full of mismatches between what you want to say, who you want to say it to, and what tools you need to do the job.

Worse yet for evangelism, if you skip right to deciding if you need a Twitter feed or a trifold brochure to reach the people you want to reach, you risk communicating effectively with only people who like what you like and communicate the way you communicate. If you look around most mainline churches, you will see that the church has been doing that for some time now. We think it's time to make a change.

Blessed Are the Acolytes

What can we say that might induce people to hear what the church has to say? Adult learning experts tell us that adults learn something new when they need to know it. People come to church, or come back to church, because they need to know something new.

When we give workshops, Jim sometimes asks people to think of Jesus standing up to give what Christians now refer to as the Sermon on the Mount. Imagine, he says, if instead of the Beatitudes, Jesus had addressed the crowd by saying, "The altar guild will meet on Tuesday evening, and the men's group on Thursday. I know we all like a little extra sleep, but we really need the acolytes here fifteen minutes before the service begins. Families, please see if you can get out the door a little earlier."

> Our job is to tell the world, and help other Christians tell the world, our stories of God and the gospel at work. It's simple, but not generally easy.

When people come to the church, they need to know something about hope, or God's love for them, or about the existence of a community of people living according to values that dispute the hopelessness and violence they see around them. Usually the thing they need to know is not the altar guild update or the annual meeting agenda. But too often, that's all our newsletters, Facebook pages, and websites tell them.

As communicators, our job is to tell the world, and help other Christians tell the world, our stories of God and the gospel at work. It's simple, but not generally easy.

For the sake of argument, let's assume that every congregation and church organization preaches the gospel. But every group is called to do that in a different way, and so to speak faithfully to your community, you need to determine what distinctive qualities—in church talk, what *charisms*—your church community offers to the world. Developing three or four messages that convey who you are and what God is calling you to do will help you focus your communications effort on producing stories, reflections, videos, and other content that express those messages and bring them to life. Key messages, in short, can help prevent your communications from devolving into an annotated calendar.

A Process for Developing Key Messages

Gather the Right People

When we lead message and audience development exercises, we like to have five to fifteen of the organization's leaders meet in person for about three hours. Sometimes, when an organization wants to develop a full communications plan, we spend the day together discussing messages and audiences in the morning and tools in the afternoon. It's useful to have a good mix of people in the room to do this work. You need enough high-level "grasstops" leaders involved to give the process credibility and have it informed by the organization's strategic direction. You also need grassroots leaders and volunteers who have hands-on familiarity with the organization's work and as much diversity as the organization can muster in age, gender, geography, race, class, and political opinion.

It is critically important to understand organizational strategy and power dynamics when you are working on key messages. We once completed an arduous morning of work with the members of a board of trustees, wrote a lengthy memo articulating their key messages and audiences, and submitted it for review. Word came back from a few key members that although we had adequately articulated what we had heard from them and their colleagues, they intended to take the organization in a different direction and were frustrated that we had not articulated messages for their new, unspoken vision. Messaging work doesn't substitute for strategic planning work, and its usefulness is likely to be greatly diminished if it becomes a playing field for leaders with competing institutional priorities or visions.

1. Structure the Exercise

We begin with prayer and introductions and outline the goal of the exercise. Key messages, we explain, are not the same as an organization's mission statement or strategic goals. Rather, key messages are the things about your organization that you believe will most interest and motivate your own members and the external audiences you hope to reach.

Sometimes key messages emerge easily from conversation, especially in organizations that have done a good job at strategic planning and have reached consensus about what corner of the kingdom their community is called to cultivate. Sometimes, however, even in well-established organizations, key messages are elusive, and eventually emerge from careful consideration of the activities to which the organization commits much of its time. At other times, key messages emerge from the group's conversation, having been previously understood on some level but never fully articulated.

When we work with churches or church organizations to determine their key messages, we usually begin by asking one or more of these questions:

- What is distinctive about your community of faith?

- What is God doing in your midst?

- What are your most compelling stories about people's spiritual and missional growth and work?

We also rule two frequently offered answers out of bounds: Do not tell us that your church is welcoming, and do not tell us that it is like a family. The first is a platitude and is too often what we gently term "aspirational." (We keep a confidential list of churches where leaders tell us in a Saturday afternoon workshop that they are welcoming and where no one speaks to us when we join them for worship the next morning.) The second, as devotees of Rabbi Edwin Friedman's family systems theory will tell you, invites unspoken and unrealistic expectations, emotional wounds, and uneasy guests. When was the last time you felt entirely comfortable walking into a gathering of someone else's family?

> Do not tell us that your church is welcoming, and do not tell us that it is like a family.

Many of us in the mainline church trip over the vocabulary of spiritual experience and divine inspiration, worried that we will sound like street corner preachers who are likely to begin forcing tracts on passersby at any moment. Usually it's possible to overcome this barrier by listening carefully to the one or two people in the room who are comfortable speaking in spiritual terms. Once others in the room understand that they have permission to speak this way, the conversation flows.

Other times, people resist shaping a message because, for them, doing so has manipulative connotations. But, like the Apostle Paul, if we believe in the truth of the gospel message, we need to find ways to proclaim it to other people in ways that they can hear. (Unwillingness to do that can actually be an act of intellectual, and perhaps spiritual, arrogance.)

2. Listen for Stories

After a few hours of discussing these questions with leaders of most congregations or judicatories, we tend to discover that the stories that most excite people—that make their faces come alive and have them stirring in their seats—are ones that happen in small rooms and groups, or outdoors, or in one-on-one conversations where few people can observe them. We will hear about awakenings and transformations that many of the leaders gathered for the conversation had no idea were happening. And almost inevitably, few of the stories, distinctive qualities, or messages the group identifies about their community appear anywhere in their existing communications.

Sometimes, too, we will hear that the most distinctive quality of a church community is a struggle that they have faced. In these situations, leaders can be reluctant to contemplate crafting a message that acknowledges difficulty or setback. Despite the fact that the central story of our faith proclaims that resurrection follows death, the church often shies away from telling stories that involve conflict or loss, even when they end in rebirth.

There is a messaging sin that plagues the church and that should be guarded against even at the risk of offending liturgists, theologians, and those who blog about spirituality. Perhaps in order to disguise our fear of plainspoken talk about God, we have constructed a maddeningly arcane vocabulary and jargon that we too often use to haze newcomers and keep our club exclusive. If your conversation about what your church has to offer is sprinkled with words like "kenotic" and "perichoresis," if you declare a commitment to "living into" an "incarnational evangelism" through which you will enter into other contexts with "Christ-likeness," then start again—quickly—and mandate the use of nothing more sophisticated than eighth-grade vocabulary.

3. Decide on Goals

During a conversation about key messages, you might discover that you have not yet answered a fundamental question about your reason for mounting a communications effort: What do you want people to *do*? Some congregations or judicatories are committed to building or rebuilding the institutional church, and their answer is straightforward—they want more people to join the church. Others, turning loose of the growth measures of the traditional church, want their communications to connect people to an online community, inspire people to participate in outreach efforts, or spur people to take part in an advocacy campaign motivated by faith. Some need to inspire nominal members to become more involved in the life of the parish. And sometimes churches have straightforward campaigns to raise money, volunteers, or advocates, and their call to action is clear.

Whatever your church's reason for wanting to communicate, you will want to state it explicitly and gain consensus among your leaders so that the people responsible for communications know their goal and how their success is likely to be evaluated. A straightforwardly logical process might dictate that determining the purpose for communications *would* be the first thing to determine. But in our experience, once people begin to tell the stories of how God is working in the lives of people in their church community, their answer about why they want to share that story can change, sometimes dramatically.

4. Decide on Tone

At some point in your messaging process, your community will confront the question of how edgy you want to be. There is a tendency in mainline church circles to back away from edginess, pointedness, and directness. We don't want to offend people. We want them to think well of us. Many of us fight against childhood cautions about discussing religion, much less authentic spiritual experience, in polite company.

We forget that people got mad enough at Jesus to have him killed. We don't think that you should necessarily develop messages that will bring the power of church and state down upon you—although sometimes Christians are called to do that—but in an effort to be nice, or to say things with which no one will disagree, it is possible to develop messages that say almost nothing at all.

In some circumstances, blandness is not a bad thing. If you are a political candidate who needs to win a majority of the vote, you have to choose very carefully whom you please and whom you don't. If you make a product for mass consumption, you may prefer that it be acceptable as opposed to distinctive so that it is considered at least palatable by as large an audience as possible. But faith is not fast food. People prefer a particular flavor, and they make their choices for very personal reasons.

> In an effort to be nice, or to say things with which no one will disagree, it is possible to develop messages that say almost nothing at all.

If you are, for example, an Episcopalian in a room of one hundred randomly selected Americans, you are, statistics suggest, the only Episcopalian. If each Episcopalian found himself or herself in such a room and took one other person out of that room with them, the Episcopal Church would double in size. What is the best way to do that—a message that is inoffensive, generally well received, offends no one, moves no one? Or a message that speaks passionately, directly, and honestly to the people whom you feel you are best able to reach? As you might guess from the way we phrase the question, our preference is for the latter sort of messaging. It doesn't work in some communities, and some people are not comfortable with it. But people remember Jonah and John the Baptist and what they said—and how they said it.

5. *Choose to Tell the Hard Stories*

As we were writing this book, we were able to work with four dioceses in the Episcopal Church who are rebuilding after their bishops and many clergy left the church for conservative Anglican groups and tried to take buildings, funds, and property with them. Although courts across the country are almost uniformly returning those assets to the Episcopal Church, legal processes are slow and many of the congregations in these dioceses have had to rebuild their congregations without buildings or budgets.

Telling the story of how they have rebuilt the church without many traditional trappings can be raw and difficult, but many people disaffected from institutional religion long to hear that church isn't about buildings. And in some cases, the people of these congregations are determined to stay together despite profound theological, social, and economic differences. In a culture where people long for alternatives to the badly polarized world of politics and media, these churches have something distinctive to offer. If your church has a similar story, or can bring itself to talk honestly about seeking new life in the midst of death, you'll find that people respond.

6. *Focus on Content*

If you're leading a message development conversation, it is usually best to gather people's ideas, key words and phrases, and stories during a meeting, and then afterward draft three or four succinct messages of two or three sentences each for leaders to review. This process can help ensure that people stay focused on ideas and stories and not on wordsmithing and writing by committee.

While it's important that your draft of key messages use words that your community finds comfortable, key messages are not meant to be carved on the lintels or reprinted in the bulletin, and so polished prose is not the goal. Instead, your key messages will serve to guide your communications plan so that you know you are devoting resources to saying what most needs to be said. In general, the health of a church is inversely proportional to the amount of time its leaders spend arguing over the placement of commas. Stay on message by staying focused on your content.

Identifying Target Audiences

You want, of course, to tell your story of faith to anyone who wants to hear it. But every congregation has certain audiences it can best reach. To craft and execute an effective communications plan, you will need to know who those people are, and what they are like. So after you have identified your key messages, you will want to define your target audiences.

Group 1: Your Neighbors

It's likely that one of your key audiences is "people like us." There's nothing inherently wrong with that, as long as you are also looking around your community. If you are the church closest to a neighborhood, an apartment building, a shelter, or a group home, God has given you those people with whom to share the good news. If that job is unfamiliar or difficult or even unsettling, it is still your job.

We know of a church next to a community college that is a haven for recent immigrants seeking to gain a foothold in the labor market. The community college has few public spaces, and the church is ideally situated to welcome these students to the community. But its congregation, which drives in from surrounding middle-class residential neighborhoods, continues to seek its new members from among their peers, and the church remains a stranger to the community college students and their families. (More about this particular situation in chapter 5.)

As you identify the audiences you most want to reach, remember that communications, done well, can have consequences:

What if you're a garden-variety, mostly white, getting older, mostly educated Episcopal church and you start communicating with your Rust Belt neighborhood that is made up of formerly grand homes now subdivided into apartments where mostly non-white, not-older, less-educated people live? And what if they start coming to church?

What if you're a church in a historically African American urban neighborhood undergoing gentrification, or becoming home to new Latino families? Or what if you invite the clients of your food pantry or soup kitchen to come to church?

What if your congregation is made up predominantly of adults—young single people, and older empty-nesters? What happens when families with noisy children show up?

Attracting new audiences to your congregation is going to have implications for your programs, your worship, and even who sits on the vestry. Because if you share the news of what God is doing in your community of faith with other people and they come to check it out, then it becomes their community of faith, too.

Group 2: Your Members

Don't forget your own members when you are thinking of key audiences. One of the most important jobs of church communications is to tell the story of the church to itself. A message-focused communications plan can help keep the church focused on its priorities, ensure that members hear and read stories about what happens in the parts of the church that they do not experience directly, and help "shut the back door"— keep people from drifting out of the church once they have come in.

If your church has a significant number of members who show up occasionally and give sparingly, you'll want to consider them as a distinct audience. The church tends to think of members and seekers as separate categories, but it's probably more like a Venn diagram. People who belong to your church in name only, or materialize only at Christmas and Easter, need to hear from you in ways that might induce them to check in more often.

As you identify your key audiences, keep in mind what you decided you want people to do as a result of your communications. Some audiences take precedence in the service of one goal and are less important in the service of others. You may want to reach college students to attract them to your Sunday evening emergent worship or your summer mission program, but it's unlikely that they'll be the target for your capital campaign.

> People who belong to your church in name only, or materialize only at Christmas and Easter, need to hear from you in ways that might induce them to check in more often.

When Audience Comes First

Sometimes, particularly in advocacy or issue-oriented work, your need to reach one audience is so overwhelming that you will want to flip the order of these exercises and consider your target audiences first. Then you'll be able to develop messages that are specifically tailored to communicate to just that audience.

We have worked for several years with the Chicago Consultation, a group of Episcopal and Anglican laypeople, clergy, and bishops founded in 2006 after efforts to secure the full inclusion of lesbian, gay, bisexual, and transgender (LGBT) people hit roadblocks at the church's General Convention.

After some analysis and conversations, leaders of the Chicago Consultation noticed that Episcopalians in what political strategists refer to as the "moveable middle" had voted against them. Why? Many admitted they were concerned that the church had not "done the theology" to show that full inclusion of LGBT people was an orthodox Christian position. These middle-of-the-road Episcopalians were also deeply worried that if they included gay and lesbian people in their church, they would get kicked out of the Anglican Communion, a confederation of churches across the world that have historic ties to the Church of England.

Once the Chicago Consultation determined that it needed to focus its attention on the "moveable middle," its messaging work became relatively easy.

Step 1: They took theological materials that had been produced over decades, if not centuries, but transformed them into formats that laypeople could read over a cup of coffee without either a brown paper wrapper or an ecclesiastical dictionary at hand.

Step 2: Then they tended fears around relationships. The Anglican Communion, they reminded people, is not a hierarchy of bishops who gather in closed rooms and issue terse pronouncements. It is the relationships we form when we pray together, study the Bible together, and work together in mission to bring about the kingdom of God. The Chicago Consultation found partner Anglicans from Africa, England, and other places who shared their passion for inclusion and welcomed them to share their message with the moveable middle of the Episcopal Church.

In 2009, after three years of prayerful, gentle, concerted communication, the movable middle—and the General Convention—changed direction and began moving once again toward full inclusion.

Tapping the Right Messengers

In the Bible, God sends just the right messenger to get the job done. Jonah, once he got out of the fish, made quick work of getting Nineveh to repent, even if he wasn't happy about it. Gabriel's visit to Mary inspired the Magnificat. John the Baptist jump-started things quite nicely for Jesus.

So once you have your key messages defined, you will want to spend some time thinking about whom you should send to deliver those messages to your target audiences. Here's a basic rule of thumb: If people's lives are being transformed by what's happening in your congregation or organization, send those people first. They might be your members or they might be your partners in mission in another part of town or another part of the globe, but they are the people who can speak with conviction about what your faith has to offer. We will talk more in the next chapter about how to capture their stories and disseminate them to the people you want to reach, but put them at the top of your list of faithful messengers.

You will also want to make sure that the most compelling voices in your church community know your messages (hopefully they've been part of the group you invited to help develop them) and are prepared to use them in their everyday lives. We recommend setting aside forty-five minutes or an hour with your leaders to get them comfortable with your messages. Rebecca believes that the most transformative human conversations take place in the produce aisle of grocery stores, and so we often have leaders practice their messages in their own words as if they were standing by the cantaloupe. "What did you do this weekend, Joe?" "Well, Fred, I helped pack groceries to distribute to the neighbors near our church who sometimes run short of food money at the end of the month. We've been doing this for twenty years. How was your weekend?"

This is not an attempt to program the way that the people in your congregation talk to their friends and neighbors. It's simply a process for letting them practice comfortable ways of talking about church when they feel called to do it. We mainliners aren't good at this; we need to practice.

Sample Editorial Plan: Stage 1

Once you have your key messages, target audiences, and messengers are defined, you are ready to begin building your communications plan. First of all, what stories or information might you use to express each of your messages?

Message

Let's say that you're part of the communications ministry at St. Egbert's, an active suburban congregation with a heart for outreach. Here are the messages you've developed:

MESSAGE 1
St. Egbert's is a community of people devoted to loving and serving God, each other, and the world. We welcome skeptics, seekers, lifelong Christians, and people exploring Christianity for the first time.

You can express this message with:

- accessible, lively information about what you believe;

- stories of members who have had a spiritual awakening or are grateful for a community in which they can ask questions;

- stories about members whose work in the world is motivated by their faith.

MESSAGE 2
Our spiritual journeys are being nurtured by strong preaching and teaching, beautiful liturgy and music, and a caring community rooted in God's love.

You can express this message with:

- material by clergy;

- material that provides a glimpse of liturgy and music;

- substantive information about books, authors, teachers, and topics of Christian education programs.

MESSAGE 3
We are committed to mission with our brothers and sisters in the city near us and other places where people are in need, and we are being transformed by that work and those relationships.

You can express this message with:

- stories of church members working with people from partner communities;

- stories of people whose lives are being transformed.

Target Audience

Next, which audiences need to hear these messages? The leaders of St. Egbert's made this list:

- families with children in our community;

- faculty, staff, and students at the nearby public university;

- people who are disaffected by restrictive religious traditions;

- people active in social justice causes.

Messenger

Who should deliver the messages? St. Egbert's came up with this list:

- former skeptics and seekers who have found a home at St. Egbert's;

❧ lay leaders, including Christian education teachers and students, choir members, pastoral visitors;

❧ clergy;

❧ mission partners in city;

❧ congregation members active in mission.

Sometimes a grid can help you see clearly what you need to say to whom. We have provided a sample grid on the opposite page.

———————

Once you have organized which messages you want to deliver to which audiences, you (and the people of St. Egbert's) are ready to choose a mix of communications tools—website, print materials, social media, signage, and so on—to get the job done. We will delve into all of these more deeply in the next two chapters.

Sample Editorial Plan

Audience	Priority Message(s)	Messengers	Tools	Timeline	Who's Responsible?
Families with children	• spiritual journeys; • caring community; • strong preaching and teaching	• former skeptics and seekers; • teachers; • clergy	[see chapters 3 and 4]	[see chapters 3 and 4]	[see chapters 3 and 4]
University community	• strong preaching and teaching; • beautiful liturgy and music; • mission	• clergy; • teachers and students; • choir; • members in mission			
Disaffected from other traditions	• welcome for skeptics, seekers, lifelong Christians and people exploring Christianity; • mission	• former skeptics and seekers			
Social justice activists	• strong preaching and teaching; • mission	• clergy; • mission partners; • mission members			

CHAPTER 3

Tools of the Trade: Websites, Social Media, and Multimedia

If you are involved in church communications, in all likelihood you are expected to have a variety of specialized skills that are rarely possessed by any one person. Newspapers have reporters, editors, graphic designers, videographers, online editors, and social media specialists, but given the tight budget on which most churches operate, you may be expected to do all of that yourself.

Corporations have web specialists, brand strategists, public relations experts, and advertising personnel, but in the church, you may be expected to have a handle on all of that, too.

Political campaigns and grassroots organizations have folks dedicated to training staff and volunteers in the effective use of communications software and technologies and supporting a far-flung network of commu-

> Corporations have web specialists, brand strategists, and advertising personnel; you may be expected to have a handle on all of that.

nity-based correspondents. And it is entirely likely that the church will expect you to do that as well.

It probably isn't possible to master all of these skills, and if it were, there wouldn't be enough hours in the day to practice them all effectively. But it is possible to grasp the basic principles for effective use of the primary communication media available to Christian communicators. Once you have accomplished that, you will be able to get a sense of what is achievable given your skills, your budget, and the skill of those who are willing to help you.

Communications technologies have developed at a dizzying pace in recent years, and any discussion of the tools of our particular trade runs the risk of being badly dated before it sees print. Yet those who understand the state of our various arts in this moment will be better able to respond to changes in the field than those who do not. In this chapter and the next, we take a look at where things stand, beginning here with websites and social media, and then moving in the next chapter to newsletters (both print and digital) and advertising.

Websites

Not long ago, to have a successful website, a faith community needed to know someone who could write code. That is no longer the case. If you can successfully save a Word document or know a teenager who can save a Word document, you can have a website. Free blogging software and low-cost content management systems can be used to produce perfectly acceptable websites that are easy to design and easy to update. There are also dazzling, custom-made products that will make first time visitors *ooh* and *aah* at your distinctive design and edgy use of art. We like to think that the same set of principles is involved in every case.

The Four Tasks of a Website

A good church website—be it for a congregation, a judicatory, or a church-affiliated organization—performs four distinct but mutually reinforcing tasks:

1. *Introduce.* The site offers an institutional profile of your faith community. It tells visitors who you are, what you do, and how they can get in touch with you. The information required for this task is fairly straightforward: location and contact information, staff and leadership directories, perhaps a mission statement, a brief history of the community, and an account of its most significant formation, outreach, and stewardship activities. On most websites, the pages that provide this information tend to be static: that is, the content doesn't change much, although pages do need to be updated to reflect the comings and goings of clergy and staff or a change of curriculum in the Christian formation program.

2. *Inform.* The site informs members and non-members about the activities of the community. This is the job of calendar entries, news and feature stories, photographs, and—for some communities—blog items. These elements keep active members in the know and allow those more loosely affiliated to check the time, date, and location of particular events. They also give the rest of the world a sense of what you do by capturing you in the midst of doing it. Multimedia elements such as podcasts and video enrich the site and can be included as a community's budget permits.

3. *Enhance.* The site enhances the spiritual life of the community by offering spiritually-themed or mission-focused sermons, reflections, and stories. It provides an opportunity to discuss these materials and other spiritual concerns via links to social media. And it reaches out to

newcomers through articles that introduce them to the community and the church.

4. *Manage.* The site performs functions that increase the effectiveness or efficiency of the community's operations. These functions may include record keeping, event registration, online giving, and targeted email communications. We are not going to enumerate all of the ways in which administrative operations can be automated, but we urge you to explore them. As a communicator, you will want to know what sorts of events your various audiences attend, what types of initiatives they have supported financially, and what sorts of electronic communications they have either signed up for or opted out of.

In chapter 2, we urged you to come up with a few simple but essential messages that you hoped to communicate about your community. Developing a website is an opportunity both to bring those messages to life and to test what you have decided to say about your community against the reality of its daily life. Do the programs that form the core of your institutional profile jibe comfortably with your messages? Or does your messaging about young adults clash with the fact that you offer nothing to attract them? If you have been honest in developing your messages, you should be able to project them to web visitors by featuring information, stories, and event promotions that make your community's values and commitments clear and appealing.

Organizing Web Content

As anyone who has ever designed or maintained a website knows, almost everyone in a community believes that their favorite activities or information should be featured on the homepage. Webmasters who accommodate these wishes employ what we call the sock drawer school of web design, so named because they end up producing a homepage that looks like a drawer full of unmatched socks. You can see every sock you own, but it may take you quite a while to find a pair. Similarly, it can take quite a while to pick one's way down a homepage filled with dozens of links that "deserve" to be featured, in order to find the one you want.

With so many activities vying for attention, how does one organize and prioritize it all? You develop an intuitive "information architecture." For those who are not technologically inclined, it can be helpful to think of this work as simply arriving at the minimum number of "top level" categories in a navigation bar that are necessary to give visitors a sense of where to start looking for the information they need. Many, if not most, church sites have too many categories through which a visitor must browse to find the proper materials. As you ponder your own information architecture, ask yourself questions like: Can the categories on children's formation, youth formation, and adult formation be grouped under a single heading?

Here is one approach to information architecture that we have found works well for many faith communities:

About Us: This category should include a brief factual description of the community, perhaps a few words about its history (although visitors are typically less interested in this than church folks think), and information about the staff and governing body. This serves much of the "Introduce" function we mentioned above.

Ministries and Programs: The site should feature one or two sections on the community's programs and ministries. In general, faith communities minister both to members (Christian formation or education, pastoral care, and so on) and to the larger world (mission programs, assisting local social services or nonprofits, engaging in advocacy, offering special arts or education programs). It can be helpful to divide what you might simply call "Ministries" or "Programs" into those two categories. However, smaller communities or those with a particularly specific focus may not need to diversify.

News: Every site needs a news section that includes a calendar. Few things convey vitality more than a calendar populated with interesting events. The news and calendar section of your site should include an archive of all of the parish's newsletters with the most recent first; a calendar with several items singled out for special attention; and feeds for your Facebook, Twitter, and YouTube or Vimeo (video) accounts if you have them.

Other: If your community has a particular calling or a signature program, this might require its own category. Large congregations with numerous services and more than one choir might want a section on worship. Cathedrals and tall-steeple congregations often need a category for arts and music. Some churches share space with the community and need a category in which to promote events that take place in that space.

A striking photograph or photo rotation can give visitors a strong sense of your parish's identity.

Contacts and Basics: Contact information, a worship schedule, and links to the calendar should be easy to find, but not necessarily in the most prominent display space. People are motivated to look for this kind of information, and arrive at your site with some confidence that they will find it. Don't hide it, but save the best display space for stories and events that convey a distinctive sense of your parish.

It is important to understand that your information architecture in no ways restricts what can appear on your home page. In general we advise a homepage that is a mix of static and dynamic items, and that incorporates art as well as text. A striking photograph or photo rotation can give visitors a strong sense of your parish's identity. A welcome message that appears beside the dominant art on the homepage invites those who are new to your community, or who are exploring it online, to learn more.

Below the main art, you can feature both stories from your parish newsletter that bring your messages alive and promotional notices about important events. Or, if you do not have a newsletter and do not sponsor many events, you can use the prime display space near your main art to introduce people to your most important ministries.

Remember that regular users of your site will quickly learn to bypass the homepage and go directly to the information they want. It is important that the homepage is designed in a way that makes it easy for them to find their way to the interior pages of the site quickly. But remember, your website is on the *Inter*net, not the *intra*net. It is your front porch, your store window. Increasingly, it is the place where church seekers will encounter you for the first time. The images you choose, the stories you tell, and the events you promote should communicate your primary message to the first-time visitor.

Beyond the Website

In the jargon of the trade, traditional websites are pull communications—you want to pull people to your site.

We were once working with a group assembled to help us develop a new website for an Episcopal cathedral. One of the younger people in the group, a man in his late twenties, said, "I'll know it is a good site if I never have to go to it." That might sound counter-intuitive at first. But think about it: The most devoted members of your congregation know when services are, how you approach youth formation, and what kind of outreach work you do. What they do not know, until you tell them, is what is going on in the community this week: whose story is being told in the e-news letter, whether the rector has written something fresh on her blog, or if the music director posted a podcast or a YouTube video.

While all of this information needs to live on the website, none of it should stay there. A young person with a smart phone who wants to keep up with your parish may want to receive information via email or Facebook or Twitter or YouTube, or an RSS feed (which alerts him electronically every time you update certain information).

The more prevalent the use of mobile devices in your organization, the more important it is that you push new information off the website and into people's phones. If your church organization yearns to attract more young people—and what church organization doesn't?—you must have a website that delivers content in these ways.

Social Media

Where the People Are

Willie Sutton supposedly said that he robbed banks because that was where the money was. Social media is where the people are. Some church folks may find it strange that we think it is necessary to dwell on the importance of platforms such as Facebook, which claimed 800 million users in September 2011, and Twitter, which analysts believe reached 500 million users by March 2012. These media tie people together across great distances and allow users to form friendships, debate issues, mobilize support, plan rallies, raise money, and otherwise move the world.

In our experience, the mainline churches have been slow to appreciate the power of these tools. If we had a dollar for every time a Twitter-resistant church leader told us that he wasn't on social media because he didn't want to know what So-and-So had for breakfast, we could have fed the five thousand from our own accounts.

In July 2012, the General Convention of the Episcopal Church passed a resolution known as the Social Media Challenge (Resolution D069). Supported primarily by forward-thinking young leaders, it "challenge[d] every diocese and congregation in The Episcopal Church to actively engage social media in its current and future manifestations." That a resolution was necessary to bring global communications phenomena to the attention of the church is evidence of entrenched resistance to social media. That this legislation won the approval of the church's House of Bishops, which does not allow its members to tweet (send Twitter messages) during its meetings, is a dollop of irony for the top of the sundae.

Some might argue that face-to-face relationships are inherently superior to anything that can be fostered online. The church, they say, cheapens itself by substituting virtual community for what they regard as the real thing. In fact, social media can be a lifeline to people who are lonely, isolated by virtue of illness or circumstance (How many evening church events did you attend when your children were toddlers?), or simply enjoy the medium as a way to talk with interesting people who live far away. If you are encountering resistance to social media because it does not meet the church's high standards, it's worth wondering if what you are really hearing is a new twist on the church's old fear of reaching out beyond our own walls to people we don't know.

> Social media are among the few ways that church groups can reach audiences that have not previously heard of them.

The truth is, social media are among the few ways that church groups can reach audiences that have not previously heard of them. They are also among the easiest ways church members have to share church information and spiritual content with their friends. Their potential as tools for invitation and evangelism are considerable, and the church ignores them at its peril.

The Big Two: Facebook and Twitter

While there is an ever-increasing number of social media, right now most communities can safely focus on Facebook, Twitter, and perhaps a video platform such as YouTube or Vimeo (more about video toward the end of this chapter, under "Content"). Elizabeth Drescher has laid the theological foundation and explored social media's potential for evangelism, spiritual growth, community building, and pastoral care in her book *Tweet If You ♥ Jesus: Practicing Church in the Digital Reformation*.[1] She and the Reverend Keith Anderson have produced an easy-to-follow guide for beginners that also provides thoughtful commentary on the strengths and weakness of various kinds of social media in *Click 2 Save: The Digital Ministry Bible*.[2] We are not going to attempt a *Reader's Digest* version of their work here. However, we do want to say a few words about the role that the three social media that are dominant as of this writing can play in your community or organizational communications plan.

Facebook and Twitter are excellent ways of broadcasting your events to audiences that do not receive your organization's communications and do not have a reason to visit your website. Post links to the best stories on your website, as well as links to upcoming events. Remember that if members of your community share these links on their own Facebook pages, or "retweet" them on Twitter, they will be seen, and perhaps discussed, by people who might not previously known that your church existed.

Bishop Jeffrey Lee of the Episcopal Diocese of Chicago once wrote an opinion article for the *Chicago Tribune*'s website about violence in Sudan. The essay was spotted and tweeted by Bono's ONE Campaign, which at that time had nearly half

---

[1] Elizabeth Drescher, *Tweet If You ♥ Jesus: Practicing Church in the Digital Reformation* (Harrisburg: Morehouse Publishing, 2011).
[2] Elizabeth Drescher and Keith Anderson, *Click 2 Save: The Digital Ministry Bible* (Harrisburg: Morehouse Publishing, 2012).

a million followers. For one afternoon, the voice of an Episcopal bishop reached a few hundred thousand people who would not otherwise have known that the church was praying and working for its sisters and brothers in Sudan.

While winning a wider audience for your news and events is a worthy aim, it only scratches the surface of Facebook and Twitter's potential.

Because Facebook makes interaction so easy, you can convene conversations on your organization's page. Think about the messages you have developed. Think about the kinds of issues the people in your organization are concerned about. Study the day's news—in the world, in the nation, in the church, in the neighborhood—with those issues in mind. Is there a news-driven conversation taking place in any of these arenas that has special resonance for the people of your community? Is there a conversation raging online to which your ministry is particularly qualified to contribute? Do people need a safe place to discuss a controversy that is roiling your community?

You can provide that space simply by linking to a news story and asking people how they feel about it. Or, your organization can mention a high profile news story and offer a bit of pastoral wisdom or prophetic provocation. If you get in the habit of asking questions, or respectfully expressing your organization's views, you may find a myriad of willing conversation partners. Establishing a reputation as a ministry that convenes vigorous online conversation not only raises your visibility, but also gives people a strong sense of your values and priorities. And once you have their attention, you can bring the full range of your organization's activities to their attention.

Twitter cannot match Facebook as a medium for hosting conversations in which dozens of individuals can discuss the same issue over an extended period of time. Twitter is much more "of the moment." However, Twitter can be a useful tool for cultivating relationships with people who are passionate about your issues and for catching the attention of influential writers and thinkers.

Many people use Twitter as a news aggregator. They can follow all of the media outlets, columnists, activists, nonprofit organizations, and community leaders whose activities interest them at a single glance. (Obviously they can follow their friends as well, but more on that in a minute.) By following these people, Twitter users are able to reply to their tweets. If you tweet links to thought-provoking material, and reply to others tweets in interesting ways, the person whom you follow may reply to you—in which case you have placed yourself on the radar screen of an influential individual. They may even follow you back, in which case you can send them private messages. As we were finishing this book, we arranged an interview for one of our clients with a major daily newspaper whose religion reporter we had gotten to know exclusively through Twitter.

Twitter is also an excellent tool for communicating with friends and strangers who are paying attention to the same event. The event may be the Super Bowl, or a street demonstration, or the governing convention of a mainline church. By following the *hashtag* created for this event you can join in a conversation that in some instances shapes the outcome of events. (A hashtag always begins with the pound sign, and includes some further identifying characters.) #GC77 was the hashtag for the 2012 General Convention of the Episcopal Church. Those who followed it were treated to real time reporting from the House of Bishops and the House of Deputies and a vigorous debate about the merits of various pieces of legislation. They also received information about hastily organized meetings, late-breaking opportunities for communal prayer, and real-time commentary from people at the convention and those following it from afar.

> Twitter is a powerful, almost instantaneous, grassroots organizing tool.

You may not foresee an immediate need to organize flash mobs for your church organization. You may not have enough folks in your parish who feel comfortable on Twitter to participate in running real-time commentary on the pastor's favorite television show. But consider that in an emergency, when information must be shared quickly among people who are quite possibly on the move, Twitter is a powerful, almost instantaneous, grassroots organizing tool. Toppling a dictator is probably not on your agenda, but it works for that too. #Arabspring

Being Present in Digital Space

One of Drescher's most significant insights is that social media are not simply means of promoting your ministries; they are means of actually *doing* the work of ministry. Forget for a moment the importance of publicizing events, or carving out a place for yourself in public conversations. Focus on the work that churches do even if no one is looking. You pray. You care for one another. You endeavor to bring the lessons of your faith to bear in your daily lives.

You can knit your community or organization closer together by making your Facebook page or Twitter stream a place where prayers are requested and offered, where significant life events are celebrated or mourned, where the lessons of scripture can be considered in the sometimes unflattering light of our daily lives. But you don't just have to wait for people to come to you. Facebook, as Drescher has pointed out, is an excellent means of paying pastoral calls on those whom you cannot visit in person.

Even something as simple as "liking" someone's Facebook status can send a message that the church cares about its members. Early in his social media career, Bishop Mark Beckwith of the Episcopal Diocese of Newark "liked" the status of a young person in the diocese. A few minutes later, one of the young person's friends left a comment. "Dude," he wrote, "I can't believe your bishop liked your status!"

Digital Ministry Standards and Practices

The best social media practices promote sustained engagement and foster relationships—just like the best face-to-face practices. If you have one person who is able to handle social media for your church organization, you know it's getting done. It guarantees consistency of voice and serves as a hedge against duplication. On the other hand, if you have several people who are able to work together, you bring varying perspectives and diverse voices, which may well be an advantage. If you are lucky enough to be able to assemble a social media team, it's important that everyone involved be clear on the organization's overall goals and messages and agree upon standards of decency and boundaries.

Many organizations and church bodies have produced social media standards, which are usually available online. We think that if you follow the basic rules of human conduct in force in the rest of the world, you will be okay:

- Don't say things to people in a way that you wouldn't want them said to you.

- Don't plagiarize.

- Don't incite violence.

- Never form private relationships with children not your own.

What frightens people about social media is often not what their church might post online but rather what someone might write in response. Recently we did a social media workshop in which we extolled the virtues of social media for ministry and pastoral outreach. During the question-and-answer time, a man in the very back of the room raised his hand and said, "But if you put things on Facebook and let people comment, then anything could happen!" Rebecca said that was exactly the point.

If you are part of your church's social media team, you want to be sure to have a system and safeguards in place so that you see all the postings on your page and messages directed to you quickly and can respond when necessary—either by deleting something inappropriate, reporting spam or online abuse, or arranging a pastoral response when someone is in crisis. But in general, social media is like any other kind of human interaction: some people will behave well and others will behave poorly.

> If kids are online, the adults who care for them need to watch like hawks for bullying, predators, and inappropriate activity.

The exception to that generosity is when it comes to protecting children. We are zealous on this front. If kids are online, the adults who care for them need to watch like hawks for bullying, predators, and inappropriate activity. But it is still true that most abuse against children happens at the hands of a family member or a close family friend. Researcher Danah Boyd and others assert that teens benefit from online activity much more than they are harmed by it, and as parents and communicators, we are inclined to agree. Fear of abuse is no reason to close the door to social media entirely.

Blogging

Many people assume blogging should be an essential part of a social media presence. We're not so sure. The word blog (a merger of "web log") has come to mean two distinct things. It is both a place where people express opinions online, and an online publishing platform that can give you a quick and easy way of establishing an online presence where you can publish writing, video, and audio content.

When should your church organization have a blog?

➤ If you are trapped in a website that is difficult to update quickly, a blog may be an easy and inexpensive stopgap measure to increase your online effectiveness while you resolve the difficulties with your website.

❧ If your organization has ongoing conversations about spiritual issues and community issues, a blog can be a good place to keep that conversation going and to broaden its audience.

❧ If one or more of your organization's key messages is focused on a specific issue, and one or more of your key audiences is deeply interested in that issue, then maintaining a blog can be just the right way to have a substantive online conversation with that audience.

The best blogs tend to take shape based on the gifts of the individuals who maintain them. You should not simply put your rector's sermons on a blog and expect a salon-style conversation to take place in the comment section. That will not happen. But if there is someone in your community with a real gift for written or spoken conversation about issues that are essential to the life of your community, they may, over time, be able to develop an audience and by doing so further your ministry. The same is true if someone in your church organization possesses an expertise that is much in demand.

In some cases, church leaders may wish to have an online outlet for writing, music, photography, or video that lies outside the established ministry of the organization. They may wish to be able to speak without being presumed to speak on behalf of the organization. In these cases, a personal blog can work well; it can be linked from the organization's website if the blogger so chooses, but it should state clearly that it is not an organizational blog and that the blogger is not speaking for the organization that she or he leads.

You can develop an effective presence on Facebook and Twitter relying almost entirely on a passion to make connections with people, and an ability to initiate and sustain conversations. But, for the most part, when it comes to blogging the best practitioners either create compelling original content, or adroitly curate content produced by others.

If you maintain a blog, you will need to decide whether to accept comments on the items that you post. Some corners of the Internet are as freewheeling as a Western saloon, and you will want to develop a policy on who is allowed to post comments and what they are allowed to say. Most blogging software allows you to read comments before you publish them. We think it is a good idea to do so. That said, some software allows you to "trust" regular commenters who keep a civil tongue, meaning that their comments can appear immediately. Jim requires commenters at Episcopal Café to sign their comments using their real names. John Q. Public tends to speak more reasonably as John Q. Public than as RatSlayer65.

> No matter how popular your blog becomes, it's likely that much of its traffic will come via social media and your email newsletter.

Don't forget to post links to your blog on Facebook, Twitter, and other social networking sites. No matter how popular your blog becomes, it's likely that much of its traffic will come via social media and your email newsletter.

Content for Websites and Social Media

Photos

As you study response to your various communications, you will likely discover that people respond well to photo albums of worship and other events. However, for people who came of age in the days when photographs and video were taken by professionals and were hard to come by on a limited budget, the popularity of online photo albums in church communications can be a bit unsettling.

It is still important to have professional, high-quality photographs for print publications and prominent online placement like website homepages. But social media platforms have become increasingly visual, and to make full use of their potential, you will want to take, collect, and post informal photos taken at worship and community events. As long as it's done with permission, the process of "tagging" photos—a simple operation on Facebook—is a good way to alert the person in the photo and everyone else in that person's network that the photo exists. By tagging your photos, you ensure that a wide audience sees images of your worship, community, and service. A robust online photo album gives your members an easy way to share their life at church with friends who may be seeking a spiritual home.

When you do need photos for print publications, make sure your photographers know that images must be run at a larger size and higher resolution in print than online, and therefore must be of a better quality. This, obviously, makes them harder to come by, and you will need to plan accordingly. Additionally, the quality of photography must correspond to the purpose of your publications. Newsletters and newspapers can get away with printing mediocre images that are primarily documentary. But the higher quality printing of a magazine requires photography that deserves to be reproduced on glossy paper. Additionally, in a publication that serves a particular purpose—supporting a capital campaign, for instance—the photos are as important in driving home the message as the text. So plan accordingly.

One way to assemble a decent photo library on a budget is to pay a professional photographer to shoot multiple images at a single gathering that can be deployed at various times throughout the year. The gathering, it follows, should not be seasonally themed because you cannot use Christmas images in Lent.

Other photo tips:

- Avoid running pictures—either online or in print—in which people's faces aren't large enough for them to be identified.

- Aim for candid shots and avoid posed group photos.

↝ Avoid, if at all possible, photographs of people looking into the camera and smiling, especially if they are shaking someone's hand (the infamous grip and grin shot) or accepting a large cardboard check.

↝ Ensure that you attend to and comply with your community's rules about using photos of children.

↝ Keep in mind that images of empty worship spaces, no matter how architecturally significant, are unhelpful unless accompanied by a story examining why no one is coming to church. Likewise, if the most compelling image you have to share with the world is of the exterior of your church building, you are telling the world something sobering about the nature of our faith.

Podcasts and Audio Recordings

If your church community enjoys particularly powerful preaching or lively education forums, you may decide to make audio recordings of these presentations and podcast them for listeners to enjoy at home or on their mobile devices. To develop a following for these audio presentations, your content needs to be extraordinarily good and the sound quality needs to ensure that listeners have no difficulty hearing over headphones, in the car, or on tiny computer speakers.

Audio recording and podcasting can be particularly successful if your pastor's preaching and teaching often addresses matters of concern to the wider community. At Trinity Episcopal Cathedral in Cleveland, Dean Tracey Lind has developed a strong following for her sermon recordings and podcasts of public radio-style adult education forums that often take on her struggling city's hot topics, like sustainable development, urban gardening, public school reform, and racism. Becoming known in the wider community as a cathedral that is deeply invested in the rebirth of the city has resulted in a steady stream of young, energetic members—many of whom haven't been to church in years, if ever.

Videos

A professionally shot and edited video can introduce your church community to new audiences and change hearts and minds in advocacy campaigns. Most communications budgets, however, allow for this sort of undertaking only once every few years, if that.

For workaday purposes, the online world has not just accepted but embraced videos taken with smartphones, hand-held video cameras, and tablets. New apps even make it possible to shoot, edit, and upload video directly from a smartphone, meaning that your email newsletter, social media channels, and website or blog can include fresh video that conveys a sense of the moment with relative ease.

> New apps even make it possible to shoot, edit, and upload video directly from a smartphone.

Videos can also help establish a church leader's personal relationship with people she has not met or does not get to see often in person. While some leaders love to write well-crafted essays for their flocks to read, others find writing a chore, and relegate it to the bottom of a long list of tasks. Some writing-averse leaders, however, will make time to use a smartphone or tablet to record posts for a video blog. Forget all but the most basic production values in these instances; the goal of these videos is to establish a direct connection, unmediated by producer or editor. Rebecca once considered editing out the end of one client's homemade video so that the audience couldn't see him reaching over to turn off the recording device on his iPad. Then an enthusiastic older woman told her that this seemingly awkward moment was her favorite part of the posts. "That's how I know it's really him!" she exclaimed.

A Note on Intellectual Property

Intellectual property law governs who owns the photos, videos, and audio recordings you post electronically. It even governs who owns the sermons your pastor preaches in church. Be sure to consult an experienced intellectual property attorney if you are unsure about what permissions you need to seek or credits you need to grant. If you decide to use stock photos, either for print publications or on your website and email newsletter, be sure that you use only images you have permission to use and grant appropriate photo credit.

———————

No matter how expertly you deploy social media, you will still run into skeptics who will tell you that they don't go on Facebook because they don't care what Mrs. Smith had for breakfast. Consider it your pastoral duty to tell them that social media are excellent tools for spreading the news of what God is doing in their midst to people who might not hear it otherwise. Tell them that social media are venues in which the feeling of belonging to a beloved community can be extended beyond Sunday morning. Tell them to get on social media and see the good work that Christians are doing there.

And then, maybe just for the heck of it, tell them what you had for breakfast.

CHAPTER 4

More Tools of the Trade: Newsletters, Print, and Advertising

In the last chapter, we discussed tools that would have been unrecognizable to communicators of previous generations. In this chapter, we will discuss how some old communications standbys like newsletters and advertising have been made new in the digital age.

How do you know when to choose new media and when to choose old? We find answering this question a little bit like deciding between a Ferrari and a tractor without being told if we'll be cruising on open highways or plowing a field. As a rule, you try to choose the right tool for your budget, and the right tool for the job. Now, let's look at what that principle looks like in practice.

The Debate: Online versus Print

Jim says on days when Episcopal Café traffic is slow, he can just post a headline saying "Let's Argue about Church Music" and stand aside. Asking church communicators about print versus online communications has much the same effect. Friend-

ships and careers can be made or broken in the debate we outline in the next few pages.

So, when do you use print and when do you use electronic
communication?

Let's start simple: On Sunday morning, or whenever your
community worships, you probably want to hand people a
piece of paper with announcements about parish life, calendar
items, and reminders of upcoming events. The emphasis here
is on refrigerator-type reminders for people already involved
in the life of the church. However, if your communications-as-
evangelism strategy works, you will have new people coming
on Sunday morning to receive these same pieces of paper. For
that reason, and because some of your members are less active
than others, you need to include information about your congregation's mission, priorities, and the events that bind it together in this material.

For life beyond Sunday morning, we offer the following
guidelines.

When to Print

1. If you are a church organization, you may well have
the need to print something about yourself for exhibits,
conventions, and other gatherings at which you will encounter people face-to-face. Be judicious. It is demoral-
izing in the extreme to wander the halls of a church
convention and see the brochure over which you labored
(and on which you spent scarce resources) stuffed in the
recycling bin.

2. You may still wish to print a newsletter or newspaper
that you mail to people's homes. Doing so will increase
the number of contacts that you have had with your audience over the course of any given month. Few people
receive all of their information through a single medium,
and it is entirely possible that someone who spends their

working life online hasn't visited the church website in a couple of months and is happy to read your print newsletter.

3. If you live in a community that allows churches to put brochures in tract racks around town, or in a community that is a tourist destination—in short, if your organization or the surrounding community receive a lot of walk-in traffic—it's nice to have a brochure, palm card, or flyer.

4. Printed pieces are useful for marking special occasions or special purposes. They are essential in fundraising campaigns. They are well suited to reaching your community with complex information that you believe is essential for them to read.

When Not *to Print*

There are many situations in which printed materials are indispensable, but there are also many church organizations publishing a print newsletter that doesn't work very well because that is what those organizations have always done. Now might be the time to rethink that practice, keeping a few things in mind:

1. Print doesn't communicate news very well anymore. If you only print and mail a monthly newsletter or newspaper, you have to accept that the method and speed with which much of your audience receives your news will be wildly out of sync with the method and speed with which it receives other kinds of news. It is better to communicate important news to your audience in more immediate ways—an email blast list, a listserv, group text messages, Facebook, or Sunday morning announcements.

2. Print isn't a very effective use of your limited budget. Printing and mailing a printed piece costs money, and in most cases is more labor intensive than electronic media.

In addition, it only reaches people who give you their mailing addresses or come to your events.

3. Print doesn't make good use of informal photos that your members take at events. In fact, getting decent art for print publications is a challenge, because images and photographs need to be reproduced at high resolution.

4. Print requires skill, and few people can competently report, write, edit, design, and layout a good print publication (and keep up the mailing list). Hiring a designer to provide you with a good email newsletter template is cost effective, and if you use software that easily integrates photographs and video clips, a generalist can turn out a sharp email publication faster and at a higher quality than a print publication covering the same material.

5. Print doesn't communicate especially well with younger Christians who are nearly always online. For a travel guide to the world of digital natives, read "Ancient Liturgy for Scruffy Hipsters with Smartphones," a profile by Jason Byassee of Lutheran pastor Nadia Bolz-Weber and her Denver congregation House for All Sinners and Saints. "The Millennials who make up the church use social media the way they use oxygen," Byassee writes. "If asked, they can discuss it. If deprived of it, they would suffer. Otherwise they don't think about it."[3]

If you are supplementing your online communications program with a print publication that includes well-written feature stories, meaningful spiritual reflections, excellent art, and just enough information about what your leadership is doing to ensure transparency, then by all means, keep doing it. But if your print newsletter or newspaper is filled with information that people read online, or needed to read online weeks ago, then it might be time to consider whether it has outlived its usefulness. If you cease to produce a regular print publication, it does

---

[3] Jason Byassee, "Ancient Liturgy for Scruffy Hipsters with Smartphones," October 18, 2011; blog.newmediaprojectatunion.org/pages/house-for-all-sinners-and-saints-article.

not mean that you cannot mail your members letters to inform them of important news, produce a seasonal event calendar, or put out a special publication if news or occasion dictates.

Hospitality Matters

We know that many communities rely on printed publications because they believe that these are the only means of reaching older members, or those who do not have adequate access to the Internet. This is a legitimate pastoral concern. However, there are only rare instances in which it should drive your communications strategy.

The church has always had members who were conversant with new communications technologies and members who were not. If the family at the end of the block didn't have a telephone, someone who did have a telephone carried a message to them. It makes far more sense, in most instances, to develop a means of getting the news you publish electronically to those who are not yet online—even if it means printing out certain stories and mailing them—than it does to continue printing a newsletter because a small number of your members do not use a computer.

> It makes far more sense, in most instances, to develop a means of getting the news you publish electronically to those who are not yet online.

Poor people are less likely to be online than are senior citizens. However, in many poor and isolated communities, people have easier access to smart phones than to print publications. Additionally, churches in those areas may not have the money to produce such publications with any regularity. In these instances, digital communications and social media, tailored to a mobile phone, are often the best option. We once asked Archbishop Thabo Makgoba of the Anglican Church of Southern Africa his advice on how to reach as wide an audience as possible with the news of a conference we were planning in his country, and he answered quickly: DVD. It isn't a hard and fast rule, but sometimes the technologies that we assume exclude poor people actually make it easier to reach them.

E-Newsletters

We think that nearly every religious organization needs an electronic newsletter, and some need more than one. Some need print newsletters as well. Regardless of whether your newsletter arrives in a mailbox or an inbox, it needs to do three things:

- ☙ tell stories that reinforce your messages by demonstrating what God is up to in the lives of the people in your community;

- ☙ promote particular events; and

- ☙ provide people with the nuts and bolts information they need as members of your organization.

1. Telling Stories

What kind of stories should you tell? Think about your key messages and the kind of stories that bring them to life: features on people's faith journeys, reports on mission initiatives, and explorations of spiritual development within your community. One particularly effective technique is to pair someone who writes well with someone who has a compelling story to tell. Rebecca once worked on a newsletter essay with a woman who had previously supported the death penalty, but had been transformed by her faith into a prayerful activist for its end. The piece received more response than nearly anything the church had ever published, and several of the heartfelt comments were from people who disagreed about the issue but were profoundly moved by the advocate's journey of faith.

In dioceses or large parishes, the e-newsletter is a good place to introduce the community to itself by doing short profiles of members. Much of the ministry of baptized people happens Monday through Friday out in the working world, and most laypeople are hungry to hear about how others connect their faith with their jobs, families, and civic responsibilities.

2. Promoting Events

Successful event promotion requires giving people a reason to add something to schedules that are already likely to be rather full. Time, date, and a brief description generally are not enough. You need to answer a single question that will formulate in every reader's mind: Why should I do this?

3. Including Nuts and Bolts

Nuts-and-bolts information can include everything from schedules and reminders to information that fosters transparency and accountability within your organization and allows members to make well-informed decisions and choose good leaders.

Best Practices for E-newsletters

E-newsletters, in particular, have the broadest reach of any communications tool that typical religious organizations can afford. Except for some people who are very old or very poor, nearly everyone has an email address. Even those who seldom sit at a computer send and receive email.

Email's effectiveness with youth and young adults is not what it once was, because they have moved on to other, more easily accessible methods such as text messaging, Facebook, and Twitter. They often think of email the way that some of us think of snail mail—as the way that part of the world we aren't interested in hearing from attempts to get in touch with us. Nonetheless, as long as email remains a primary tool for business and education, we expect that email will remain a broad-based communications tool.

To be most successful, your e-newsletter needs to be entirely integrated with your website. The stories and content featured in your e-newsletter should live on your website so that you can feature short excerpts (and a compelling photo) that will draw readers to click and read the whole story. Good email newsletter programs—we like Constant Contact, which is something of an industry standard, but there are others—provide templates that will allow you to lay out a newsletter that features the first paragraph of a number of items, one below the other, accompanied by links to stories on your website, video on your YouTube or Vimeo pages, photos on your Flickr or Facebook page, and RSS feeds from blogs or other websites with reliable church news, inspiring spiritual content, or other information that your readers will find interesting.

If you're new to email newsletters, here are a few helpful things to remember as you develop your template:

- Use a one-column format that can be easily read on a smartphone or tablet—that's how many of your readers will view what you send.

- Use thumbnail images for as many articles as possible. These will break up your copy and entice the scrolling reader to pause and click.

- Make your articles short and provide people a link to your website to read the entire article, find out more details, or see a photo album.

- Embed video clips so that people can watch them from within the newsletter, and keep them short (under three minutes is good; under two minutes is better).

- Give people a handy reference for upcoming events by including a list of those events in each issue of the newsletter. Make the name of each event a hotlink to a description of the event on your website.

❧ People will not scroll through yards of screen—they'll give up and the news at the bottom of your newsletter likely won't get read.

❧ Change your subject line each issue to give people a new reason to open your email.

❧ Push a link to your email newsletter out on Facebook and Twitter so that you reach people who aren't email subscribers and people (particularly young people) who get their information primarily through social media.

❧ Archive issues of your email newsletter on your website so that they are available to seekers, newcomers, and leaders who need to review past material.

Talk of embedded videos and RSS feeds can be daunting to a newsletter editor or church secretary who has spent years laboring over a print newsletter. It's worth remembering that nearly everyone over the age of thirty-five has a learning curve when making the transition to online platforms. Keep in mind that good online tools, like e-newsletter utilities, provide help videos, tutorials, and online training and assistance. If your church community is just wading into online communications, you will need to allow for some time and training of staff and volunteers who are responsible for the effort. The most popular online tools, however, are generally the most intuitive, and once the initial intimidation wears off, you'll likely find that you know, or can guess, much more about how they work than you might have expected.

Specialized Newsletters

Many large church communities will need more than a general e-newsletter. In particular, it is often helpful to have a separate e-newsletter aimed at the organization's leadership. This might well be a publication that deals primarily in keeping community

leaders up to date in an efficient fashion on impending deadlines, new resources, and governance or administrative concerns. However, it is also an opportunity for the leader of your
organization to give this important audience a pep talk or seek
its suggestions on particular issues. The e-newsletter will have
a higher readership if recipients know that there is both a re-
ward for reading it and a consequence in the form of a missed
deadline or opportunity if they do not read it.

Large communities also might need e-newsletters for participants in particularly popular programs. As a person responsible for communications you will seldom want to create a
special e-newsletter for a program that doesn't have a large audience, and you will want to be careful about authorizing volunteers over whose work you have no control to publish
material under the organization's name. Nonetheless, there are
times when a certain initiative deserves and requires its own
publication with a distinctive banner, voice, and editorial plan.
Youth ministry is probably the most common example, but outreach to young adults and those whose primary language is not
English are particularly important for many churches.

Evaluating Readership

Remember when we used to pretend that each household on
our print subscription list plucked our publication out of the
mailbox, sat down to read it thoroughly, and then placed it
prominently on the coffee table for friends and neighbors to
see? One of our favorite aspects of e-newsletters is that good
programs, like many social media platforms, provide nearly immediate, extremely detailed, and dispassionately accurate metrics about whom you are reaching and what information
interests them most.

Whether you're launching a new e-newsletter or have had
one for years, you can nearly always improve your editorial plan
through a regular review of your opening rate (how many people open your emails) and click-through rate (how many people

click your link to your website, video pages, social media networks). Best of all, metrics help balance the biases inherent in reader feedback, which can be skewed both by people who are too nice to tell you what they really think and people who rise in the morning looking for a reason to complain.

Over time, if you pay attention to metrics and feedback, you will figure out what kind of stories appeal to your audience. People will nearly always click through most to news, photos, or videos about their friends and colleagues and stories about people in the community. If the stories at the top of your email get much more attention than those at the bottom, it's likely that your newsletter is too long. Often this problem can be solved by making the last item in your email a regular feature that people are drawn to and learn where to find: alumni or member news, fresh updates via RSS feed from a blog or news site, or a photo album.

These metrics also make life a little easier for communications people when members of the clergy rush up to them, usually in front of the bishop or executive, and declare that they are not receiving any information from the diocese. With a few keystrokes you will be able to ascertain if this is true or not, and if, as is often the case, these people have in fact received and opened numerous e-newsletters from you.

Print Newsletters and Other Print Materials

Online communication has many advantages, but for on-site use and breadth of reach, you will likely want to continue to use print in some format. A few basic principles pertain:

Layout and Format

➤ You will want an attractive flag (the banner that goes across the top of the front page) to brand your publication.

❧ Laying out a print publication consists primarily of artfully arranging rectangles so that they cover the page. It is important to have at least one art element on every page, or, in the absence of art, something that saves the page from consisting entirely of columns of text.

❧ It is seldom necessary to use more than three fonts: one font for body type, one for headlines, and another, to be used sparingly for accents, subheads, possibly pull quotes, and other special circumstances.

❧ A debate rages around whether body copy should be set in sans serif type (a font without curled or "serif" tails). We believe it should not, but realize that this opinion will incite argument.

Content

There is frequent discussion in church organizations about whether the pastor's or bishop's/executive's column should always appear on the front page of the newsletter. We believe this is seldom appropriate in newspapers (the front page should be devoted to the most important news and compelling images you've got) but may be acceptable in congregational newsletters. However, we prefer publishing such a piece in a designated and unchanging space inside the newsletter, perhaps on page 2.

In considering how best to communicate with your members and the wider community, a little bit of organizational self-awareness is important. If you cannot produce a decent printed newsletter, you should try another medium. We know of an organization that not long ago switched from a mediocre newspaper to a competent quarterly magazine. The resulting uptick in readership and enthusiasm was used as a way to argue the value of magazines over newspapers rather than simply to acknowledge that good communications vehicles are more likely to be consumed than poor ones.

If you are one of the few church organizations that has a truly excellent newsletter or newspaper, the quality of that publication may be a reason to continue producing it, rather than switching to an Internet-dominated approach. Its quality may be such that it is attracting readers who would normally prefer electronic communications.

Advertising

Churches' needs for advertising generally fall into three broad categories: identity ads, special event ads, and Christmas and Easter ads.

1. Identity ads feature your name and something about your values, including the ubiquitous announcement that "The Episcopal Church Welcomes You." An edgier version is "Christ died to take away your sins, not your mind." Or "It's called baptism not brainwashing," or "God Loves Everyone. No Exceptions." These ads can be excellent for launching or reinforcing a new identity or counterbalancing campaigns by more restrictive religious traditions or, much worse, hate groups.

2. Special event ads can be helpful when you are doing something that might truly be of interest to people who are not members of your organization. This might include hosting a speaker or performer who is known outside the church, holding a community holiday meal, or serving as the venue for a meeting, exhibit, or concert of note. Before you place an ad (or solicit news coverage), however, be sure that you want visitors and are ready to receive them. We know of a congregation that got great visibility for a community party it was hosting, but when people from a neighboring congregation arrived, no one spoke to them.

3. On Christmas and Easter, many people who do not usually go to church go to church. You can advertise to

bring them in with promises of a lively children's service, a stirring sermon, or excellent music. But if you aren't ready to offer them a genuine welcome even in the midst of holiday rush, you are simply renting a pew by the hour for whatever they throw in the plate. Any connection they will form with you will be accidental, not intentional, and you might have wasted your ad budget. So buy the ad, but do the follow-through, as well.

Save Your Advertising Dollars

In the past many churches bought ads in the Yellow Pages and some bought ads in the Saturday religion section. We do not think either of these is a good use of money for most parishes. Few people use the phone book at all anymore, much less to shop for churches. And readership of print newspapers is dwindling fast in nearly all demographics. Many newspapers do not even have a Saturday religion section anymore.

There may be an argument for taking out an ad on the Saturday religion page if you are in an area frequented by tourists, or if you are doing something that will really appeal to church people from other traditions or congregations. This may include hosting a speaker who is well known in church circles—what we jokingly refer to as "church famous." Since many of the people who read religion pages are church people looking to see which other churches place ads, you may find it necessary to raise the flag there periodically (perhaps for Christmas and Easter) to keep your own constituency happy. And you may have the opportunity to draw church music aficionados who church hop each week depending on who's got Fauré and who's got Rutter. But is that the crowd you want to spend money to catch and release? It's not evan-

> Advertising in the traditional manner requires you to pay to reach people who can't or won't respond.

gelism, and in an era of shrinking budgets, we don't think it is worth it.

Perhaps the biggest drawback to advertising in the traditional manner is that it requires you to pay to reach people who can't or won't respond. This is especially true in major media markets in which you may have to pay to reach hundreds of thousands of people who live nowhere near your church (and wouldn't come even if they lived closer), all in an effort to reach the far smaller number who might be in a position to respond. If your only option for advertising is in mass circulation media, consider partnering with other congregations in your area or with your judicatory.

Money Well Spent

We think most church organizations are best served if they forego major media outlets and look for ways to target their advertising as precisely as possible. Community newspapers are more likely to be read cover to cover than thick metro dailies, and they reach fewer people who live a great distance from your church. Advertising on the websites of your local newspaper and radio station can reach much the same target market. Your local high schools may sell advertising in the programs for their theatrical presentations or on the fence at their baseball games. Well-situated billboards can be useful, particularly in an area with a minimum of visual clutter to compete for people's attention.

The radio market is extremely fragmented, so unless your church feels a particular calling to evangelize the easy listening set or the urban contemporary market, we recommend all-news stations that often have the most listeners and the broadest demographic reach. It is also possible, with some patience and creativity, to craft underwriting messages for public radio stations that convey your message without running afoul of the FCC. If you do feel called to evangelize the urban contemporary market, or any other demographic that can roughly be defined in relation to the playlist of a radio station, then commercial radio is definitely your medium.

The advertising opportunities that show the greatest potential for cash-poor church organizations are Facebook and Google. On Facebook, you can target your ad both geographically and by making it visible only to those who have "liked" pages that would indicate that they have an interest in or affinity for your community or the event it is promoting. On Google and other search engines, this work is done by the search terms you use. These platforms not only allow you to target your advertising but also allow you to cap your costs by taking your ad offline after it has been viewed or clicked on a certain number of times. Facebook can also indicate whether a particular page has been "liked" by any of your friends, thus including a recommendation from someone you may know and trust in the presentation.

If you are going to spend money on an ad, make sure that you can afford an eye-catching design that is easily readable and contains only the information required to get people to your website and location. In all but the most expansive ad, you can give people a single concept—we are open-minded Christians; we are artsy Christians; we really care about families—and contact information, including your website. Anything else probably runs the risk of producing a cluttered display that people either won't take time to read, or will note as evidence that your church lacks certain basic competencies.

Revisiting the Editorial Plan

Stage 2: Choosing the Right Tool for the Job

Once you have surveyed the communications tools available and your budget and human resources, you can choose how best to deliver your messages to your audiences using the right messengers. Here's the editorial plan grid-in-progress from St. Egbert's, our mythical congregation from chapter 2, updated to include the tools just discussed:

Updated Editorial Plan

Audience	Priority Message(s)	Messengers	Tools	Timeline	Who's Responsible?
Families with children	• spiritual journeys; • caring community; • strong preaching and teaching	• former skeptics and seekers; • teachers; • clergy	• video blog; • members' spiritual reflections; • online calendar of education programs		
University community	• strong preaching and teaching; • beautiful liturgy and music; • mission	• clergy; • teachers and students; • choir; • members in mission	• audio recordings of sermons and music; • seasonal guide to programs; • video interviews of members who do mission		
Disaffected from other traditions	• welcome for skeptics, seekers, lifelong Christians and people exploring Christianity; • mission	• former skeptics and seekers	• essays by and videos of members asking hard questions		
Social justice activists	• strong preaching and teaching; • mission	• clergy; • mission partners; • mission members	• articles and essays about education programs; • sermon recordings; • stories and videos about mission and advocacy programs		

Stage 3: Getting It Done. On Time

To ensure that your editorial plan sees action rather than dust bunnies, you will need to develop a realistic timeline that rotates attention on your priority messages as the liturgical season and program calendar dictate and provides for some "evergreen" stories that can be featured when other content is scarce. Finally, you will need to do a clear-eyed reality check of your volunteer and staff capacity by assigning responsibility for identifying and producing content directed at each audience.

At the imaginary St. Egbert's, clergy and volunteer committee chairs work with the staff person responsible for communications to identify stories, members who can provide meaningful essays and video reflections, and information about upcoming programs and activities. The communications staff person then takes those ideas, produces the content, and distributes it according to the plan. The table on the opposite page shows how the St. Egbert's plan reads when complete.

With some creative attention and periodic review, your editorial plan grid can be a simple tool to help ensure that the rotation of content on your website, in your e-newsletter and print materials, and on your social media channels reaches all of your key audiences with news, stories, and event promotion that will lead them to know, and perhaps yearn for, what God is doing in your midst.

Completed Editorial Plan

Audience	Priority Message(s)	Messengers	Tools	Timeline	Who's Responsible?
Families with children	• spiritual journeys; • caring community; • strong preaching and teaching	• former skeptics and seekers; • teachers; • clergy	• video blog; • members' spiritual reflections; • online calendar of education programs	• priority in August–September; • January	• Christian education chair working with communications staff person
University community	• strong preaching and teaching; • beautiful liturgy and music; • mission	• clergy; • teachers and students; • choir; • members in mission	• audio recordings of sermons and music; • seasonal guide to programs; • video interviews of members who do mission	• priority at Christmas, Easter; • seasonal guide in August, January; • mission focus before summer mission trip, holidays	• clergy; • Christian education chair; • music director; • mission committee chair working with communications staff person
Disaffected from other traditions	• welcome for skeptics, seekers, lifelong Christians and people exploring Christianity; • mission	• former skeptics and seekers	• essays by and videos of members asking hard questions	• Advent, Lent	• clergy; • communications staff person
Social justice activists	• strong preaching and teaching; • mission	• clergy; • mission partners; • mission members	• articles and essays about education programs; • sermon recordings; • stories and videos about mission and advocacy programs	• year-round with focus on evergreen stories that can be used when space permits	• Christian education chair; • advocacy committee chair; • mission committee chair working with communications staff person

CHAPTER 5

Extra! Extra!: Working with the Media

Every now and then we hear people in the church say something like this: "The media only pay attention to the sensational stuff. They love conflict. They never focus on all of the good things we do." To which we have four replies:

1. The church is frequently in conflict—it has been since Paul faced down Peter at the Council of Jerusalem—and its conflict over important social issues is significant to the wider society. The media's attention is evidence that the church still matters. Be glad for it.

2. There isn't a designated mainline Protestant slot in the paper that would be filled by a story about your food pantry if arguments about sexual morality were suddenly resolved.

3. Sometimes the church does something egregious and needs to be held accountable just like any other institution. Because people rightly hold the church to a higher standard than other institutions, there is a deeper sense

of discontinuity when church folk go wrong, and that increases the news value of the story. Call it the hypocrisy factor.

4. If the media isn't telling the stories you want told it is possible (we say very gently) that those stories aren't interesting or significant enough to warrant coverage. Or, it is possible that you are not presenting them to the media in a way that catches their attention. Or perhaps you have not presented stories to the media at all.

In this chapter, we will explore ways of getting the media to pay attention to your community. We know there are times that the media pays very close attention and you wish they wouldn't. We talk about those kinds of situations in our chapter on crisis communications.

Tips of the Trade

It isn't easy to get your congregation, diocese, conference, or other sort of Christian organizations into the newspaper or in online media outlets unless something has gone significantly wrong. It is even harder to get it on television or the radio. So we begin with some tips of the trade.

Tip 1: Know what's free.

Many newspapers have free listings. Many websites have free calendars. Submitting brief descriptions of your items to these lists takes very little time, and editors sometimes troll the listings to select featured items.

Tip 2: Know what kind of stories a particular media outlet runs, and pitch them accordingly.

Does it do all news, good and bad? Does it feature fun things? Does it focus on big issues and illustrate them using local examples? Or is it a local paper that writes about community news and events and will often take your photograph and cutline— or even your well-crafted press release—and print it verbatim?

Know what kind of stories a particular media outlet runs, and pitch them accordingly.

The best and most effective way to get a grasp of how the reporters, editors, and producers at the news outlets in your community think is to read the publication, visit the website, or watch or listen to the broadcast regularly. As you do this, ask yourself what kinds of decisions were made to produce the stories that you read or hear.

Tip 3: Know the media outlet's approach to religion.

When reading a newspaper or magazine, pay attention to what kinds of stories have been written about other church organizations. Make a note of what issues seem to be of particular importance to the publication and consider ways in which your church's priorities are pertinent.

In particular, note whether the publication's coverage of religion is primarily about church politics and the church's role in politics, or whether it also includes feature stories. A story about your youth group's campout to raise awareness of homelessness is a great pitch to a reporter who wants feature story content, but not to a reporter whose coverage is primarily about theological disputes over sexuality or reproductive rights. In addition, don't limit yourself to the religion pages (assuming the publication still has them). If your organization is actively involved in a community issue, pay attention to what the reporter covering that issue writes. You might have the chance to get your organization's name and its message into a part of the paper read by people who avoid stories about religion.

Tip 4: Know the personnel.

Who covers your issue or your geographic area? What's the best way to get to know this person? If a reporter gets to know you as a reliable, responsive, and fair source, sometimes you will have the opportunity to point that reporter to people in your organization who are experts on a particular topic, or to give the reporter perspective on a story that might help shape his or her coverage. This will not always get the name of your organization mentioned, but it will build a relationship that will stand you in good stead.

Tip 5: Know what reporters need.

It's easy enough to understand what *you* get out of a reporter doing a story on your pancake breakfast or your church's fiftieth anniversary, but what does the reporter get out of it? Reporters are looking for stories whose distinctiveness can be explained to their editors in two or three short sentences. If you can't help them formulate those sentences, you can't get your story covered. Additionally, reporters may also consider whether a story can be done quickly (so they can get home,

> Reporters are looking for stories whose distinctiveness can be explained to their editors in two or three short sentences.

or get on to their next assignment); whether it is likely to get good play in their publication or on their show; whether they enjoy the experience of reporting and producing or writing the story; and whether it means something to them personally.

Tip 6: Offer a good photo-op.

For small websites or newspapers, a good photograph is often enough. Stories that no one would think of covering can find their way into a community or local news source if there's an arresting image of good quality to liven up a dull web or print page. You will have better luck placing stories that are visually compelling—talking heads, anniversary celebrations, and check presentations are not.

Tip 7: Know their style.

If you are pitching a story to the kind of publication that might take your press release, make life easy for them by writing the press release in their style. Put the essential information in the first paragraph and refrain from superlatives: don't sound like a cheerleader or an advertising copywriter. Know that you're writing for their audience: don't refer to congregational leaders using obscure titles that the editor won't be able to decipher, or use church language that is not commonly known (nave, sacristy).

Tip 8: Take the "relations" in media relations seriously.

Cultivate a professional relationship with relevant reporters. If they make mistakes, correct them diplomatically and in private; if you want to argue with the tone of coverage, do so privately. If you plan to write a letter to the editor disputing something they've written, tell them that yourself and ahead of time. Return their calls promptly and get them information they need quickly. They don't like to work late any more than you do.

Take care not to overhype your events. If you tell a reporter a certain event or development is extremely important, or that a certain speaker is a leader in their field, or that you are expecting a huge crowd at your event that night and these things turn out not to be true, the reporter will rightly mistrust you in the future.

Tip 9: Respect the reporters' time.

Television news programs are brief, competition for airtime is intense, and deadlines are tight. Stories that take place either near the station, a bureau, or at a location from which the station frequently does remote broadcasts may be more likely to get covered than those that require lengthy round trips to the event and then back to the studio.

Tip 10: Know your market.

The country is filled with small news websites and newspapers that will write a story about the departure of your old rector and the arrival of your new one, but no major urban daily is going to cover that story unless one of the said rectors is famous or infamous.

The evolution of Patch.com and other online micro news sites opens up opportunities that did not previously exist for placing stories that might not be considered significant enough to be published in a daily newspaper or covered on television. Patch reporters and bloggers work in a culture that tends to be more interactive than reporters at traditional newspapers, which, in some instances, will mean they are more willing to communicate with representatives of smaller organizations online and to take your concerns seriously. In some online news operations, reporters and producers are expected to churn out numerous stories in a day. That can work to your advantage because it makes them more reliant on organizations that can provide releases, leads, or interview opportunities that are quickly converted into stories.

You may have a difficult time getting attention on the radio unless your market has an all-news radio station or a public radio outlet that does local news. If you live in a market that does have such outlets, remember that economy of words and memorable phrase-making is as essential to good radio as striking images are to good television. Be sure to know your local stations' programming; some all-news stations still have a designated time spot for reflections by faith leaders.

News Pegs

No matter how splendid the story you pitch to a reporter or producer might be, it is unlikely to get covered if it does not have a news peg. A news peg answers two questions: why this story, and why now? The answer to the first question is sometimes more important than the answer to the second. But, in most cases, you are best served if you can persuade the media that the story you are pitching is not only important, but also of the moment.

> A news peg answers
> two questions:
> why this story,
> and why now?

Peg 1: The Superlative

Is whatever you are pitching the first, the biggest, the most? Is there something so inherently significant about what you're doing that it deserves coverage in its own right?

Peg 2: The Trend

Do you have a story that exemplifies a trend that people are just beginning to pay attention to, or that brings to light a significant development that has not yet been understood? Failing that, does your story give a local example of a larger trend, or provide a local angle on a global or national news story?

Peg 3: The Local Angle

Is your organization playing a bit role in a larger story that the media is already covering? For example, are you hosting a prayer breakfast in support of a local ballot initiative, or sponsoring a community forum on youth issues?

It isn't always essential to persuade reporters and producers that your story must be covered right this instant. There are certain kinds of features that can be published or broadcast at almost any time. Journalists refer to these stories as "evergreen." Usually, these stories appear not because events force them into print or onto the air, but because papers, websites, and radio and television programs like to leaven the news mix with a story that might strike an emotional chord.

We are speaking here of the traditional human-interest story, the tale of an individual or organization that has overcome great odds or made an unusual sacrifice for the greater good. Stories that are poignant, funny, heartbreaking or uplifting have the power to touch readers or viewers emotionally and draw them to your church. Pitching these stories is a hit-or-miss proposition, but when you hit, they can be powerful tools for evangelism. Keep an eye out for a local columnist or commentator—perhaps a radio personality—who specializes in these kinds of stories. Small towns often have them; they are more endangered in large cities.

Getting Your Voice Heard

Church leaders are used to writing sermons, but when they need to speak to a larger and more diverse audience that does not necessarily share either their faith or acknowledge the value of their theological expertise, they sometimes stumble. Yet, if the church is called to assist in the construction of the kingdom of God, to transform creation, to make the broken whole, or any of the other lofty phrases we sometimes use, it is hard to imagine how that can happen if we are absent from public debates on essential social, political, and cultural issues. Here are a few ways that you or the leaders of your organization can make your voice heard.

Op-eds

Op-eds used to be shorthand for opinion pieces that ran in daily newspapers on the page that was opposite the editorial page, on which the papers' own opinions appeared. But the meaning of the phrase has expanded and is now synonymous with "column" or "opinion piece." We continue to use the word op-ed because it connotes not just a style, but a length, and it also imposes a discipline. An op-ed piece is generally between 650 and 800 words, and that is probably the limit of the attention that the average well-informed reader is likely to give your opinion, no matter how complex the issue, nuanced your thinking, and felicitous your prose.

To increase its chances for publication, an op-ed should express a clear opinion and back it up with information, experience, or examples that are specific to the author and establish him or her as an authority on the topic. It doesn't hurt if the author's title or background suggests either expertise in the subject, or the ability to mobilize a significant organization. When drafting an op-ed, it is essential to remember that you are speaking to readers who may not be church people. You must eliminate church jargon and insider shorthand and explain any technical detail that is specific to the issue in order to get published.

Placing an op-ed online is easier than placing one in print. There is simply more space available on a newspaper's website than in its pages, and there are many new outlets—from Patch.com on the micro-local level to the Huffington Post and similar outlets that reach a national and even international audience. Your article may not be seen by as many readers online as in print because online readers can find their way directly to the content that interests them without leafing through an entire publication. However, the readers you do reach are likely to be more interested in your article, more likely to live outside the paper's circulation area (which is sometimes advantageous), and more likely to respond to it than the average newspaper reader. Additionally, the person who reads an opinion piece online has an opportunity to share it more or less immediately through Facebook, Twitter, and email. All of this can be enormously helpful if you are seeking to mobilize either support or resistance for a particular cause.

Sometimes your organization will identify a few particular issues on which it hopes to be heard. It can be helpful to have op-eds on these issues already prepared so that when the news turns in your direction, you can add a fresh opening to your article that makes reference to recent developments and send it off. For example, if you are writing about violence against children, you can prepare an essay that cites the troubling statistics, explains governmental and social failures to come to terms with the problem, and illustrates the sad consequences. Then you can save that file until the next time an outburst of mayhem takes a young life, write an opening paragraph on the most recent outrage, and send it off in an instant. Too often, in the time it takes to write an op-ed from scratch and get it approved, the window for placing it may close.

> Have op-eds on these issues already prepared so that when the news turns in your direction, you can add a fresh opening and send it off.

News Conferences

Political leaders make frequent use of news conferences to reach numerous media outlets through a single appearance. In general, these events work best if you find it necessary to speak to so many reporters that you cannot speak to them individually, or if you want to create the impression that you are up to something significant by demonstrating your ability to attract the media. They are also helpful if you have assembled a coalition—perhaps an ecumenical or interfaith community group—and need to give numerous leaders the opportunity to speak.

There are a few significant potential pitfalls to holding a news conference. The most obvious is that no one will show up. The second is that reporters often feel less well served by a news conference than by an individual interview. Another is that the news conference often feels more like a performance and less like a conversation to the person answering the questions, and church leaders may find this unnerving. Fourth, you don't have the ability to control the flow of questions at a news conference, and the event can take on a life of its own.

The advantage of a news conference is that it makes efficient use of your leader's time and creates the sense that your organization is important enough to command the presence of a crowd of reporters. Also, you may benefit from the pack mentality that prevails in some situations. A journalist who planned to ignore you may show up if he or she knows the competition plan to attend. In general, we think church news is best handled through one-on-one interactions with the media, but that isn't a hard and fast rule.

Media Training

If you or the leader of your organization is going to speak to the media, either in a one-on-one interview or at a news conference, it is usually beneficial to do some media training. Many church leaders resist media training. They are possibly quite skilled at talking to people, quite practiced in expressing their views in public, and possibly concerned that training will make them seem self-conscious or inauthentic.

But a media interview is not a conversation, and the goal is not to form a personal relationship with the reporter. Additionally, while sources have more power than they realize when giving an interview—you can't be accurately quoted on what you do not say—the reporter is the one asking the questions. So train and interview with care.

1. *Distill Your Ideas*. To begin preparing for an interview, distill your ideas in short statements easily understood by

someone not familiar with the technicalities of the issues in which you specialize. If you are going to speak to the broadcast media, practice sound bites. It isn't hard to practice for a television appearance using only a flip camera or an iPad. Have someone ask you questions and answer them. Then look at your performance.

2. *Check Your Presentation.* Did you look physically comfortable, or are you sunk so deep into your chair that you are practically folded in half? Did you sit relatively still, or did you bob and weave? Did you maintain eye contact with the interviewer? (Don't look straight into the camera.) Is your resting face (the one you wear when you aren't speaking) alert and friendly, or do you narrow your eyes and furrow your brow? Do you telegraph the end of your answers by looking away, pursing your lips, or tilting your head to one side?

3. *Review Your Performance.* After you get a sense of how you look, focus on what you said. Did you get your point across, or were you so eager to accommodate the reporter that you allowed that person to lead you off into other topics?

Did you repeat negative language in a question? If the reporter asks you if the mainline churches are in an ever-accelerating death spiral and you say, "The mainline churches are certainly not in 'an ever-accelerating death spiral...,'" then what will remain in the public's mind is "ever-accelerating death spiral."

Did you use jargon that will confuse listeners or make them turn you off? It can be helpful to include a friend who is not a church person in your practice session. She or he can let you know easily if you're making sense to a broad audience.

4. *Stay on Message.* Some media consultants recommend turning every question you are asked back to your messages. We agree in concept, and this can frequently be

done gracefully through techniques sometimes called bridging and pivoting. These techniques amount to what an English teacher in your distant past called a transition sentence.

You have probably seen these maneuvers in action. A reporter asks a pointed or accusatory question and the interview subject says: "That's one way of looking at it, but our organization has always...," or, "I prefer to think of this as...," or, "There are a wide variety of opinions on this issue, but we can all agree that...."

To take an example that will resonate within most mainline denominations: "I believe the focus on this argument among bishops in the Anglican Communion holds us back. What we really need to be talking about are the relationships that bind us together, regardless of our position on [insert issue here]. Our community is deeply involved in cultivating those relationships."

5. *Tell It Straight.* While we teach our clients to bridge and pivot, and admire those who do it well, it isn't helpful in the long run to be unresponsive to reporter's questions. Rather, we recommend anticipating those questions, and formulating factual answers. Give those facts. Don't go beyond the facts.

If you are doing a live broadcast interview, and the reporter asks a question that includes erroneous assertions, begin your answer by saying something like: "Leaving aside for the moment some of the assertions on which your question is based..." and then give your factual answers. If you are doing a print interview or a taped interview, don't answer the question, but tell the reporter, respectfully, that you believe they have some misinformation, and offer your corrections.

6. *Take Your Time.* Remember that unless you are doing a live interview, you can always pause to collect your thoughts before answering a question. Remember too

that if you aren't ready to talk to a reporter, you can always ask them their deadline and promise to call them back.

7. *Be Prepared to Give Background.* Often, having prepared for an interview, anticipated difficult questions, and practiced how to answer them, you will find yourself speaking to a reporter who has no particular knowledge about your organization or about the church. It is particularly common to get a local television reporter who is a generalist, a reporter covering a Sunday morning story who simply drew the short straw for the weekend shift, or a reporter who has no familiarity at all with the form of Christian worship or the basic tenets of the faith.

Additionally, a reporter without much religion background may have assumptions based on the religion that is dominant in your area of the country. If that dominant church is Catholic or evangelical, you may have to spend some time talking to the reporter about when your church started ordaining women and the fact that members actually vote on important church decisions. If you prepared for a harder, issue-oriented interview, you can sometimes be caught off-guard when you have to back up and give a quick version of Mainline Church 101. Shift gears. Go into teaching mode. You aren't going to turn the reporter into an expert in the course of your interview, but if you imagine yourself talking to an interested seatmate on a plane flight, or some other polite but uninformed interlocutor, you will usually come out okay.

In all instances make sure reporters know that they can get back in touch with you to check facts.

Turn Every Invitation into an Opportunity

In addition to the media opportunities that you create for yourself and your organizations, you may also have opportunities presented to you. They might not be the ones you are seeking, but they are still a means of reaching audiences you cannot reach otherwise. Invitations to speak with media representatives of organizations with strict ideological positions should be treated carefully, but it seldom makes sense to reject an opportunity to speak with a reporter from a legitimate mainstream media outlet.

The media may be interested in writing stories about your church that you do not think are important, or that you do not think are likely to result in helpful exposure. In particular, many people in mainline churches complain about the coverage devoted to controversy within the church about human sexuality, and wish that the media would focus on other issues. Some go so far as to refuse to speak about human sexuality, even after their church has made significant decisions on that issue, preferring to lecture the media on the issues they should really be covering. This is spectacularly unhelpful. If this is the opportunity the media offers you to preach the gospel—whichever side of the issue you find yourself on—preach it rather than focus on the opportunity you were not given.

> If this is the opportunity the media offers you to preach the gospel, preach it.

Any time you manage to get yourself or your church organization written about or covered in the broadcast media, it is important to have realistic expectations about the end result. On television, only tiny snippets of what you said will air. Don't be surprised to spend one or two hours with a reporter and find that they use only fifteen seconds of your interview in the final report. Very few television news stories run more than three minutes.

Likewise, you may well spend an hour or more providing background and perspective to a print reporter, only to find that you have one short quotation in the published story. Never complain, especially in public or on social media, about how little space or airtime you were given. It's a rookie mistake, and you may well diminish your credibility with the reporter and with more seasoned media commentators. However dismissed you feel at press time, your time has not been wasted: you have likely helped the reporter better understand the issue; you have established yourself as a reliable commentator; and you have built stronger relations that will serve you and your ministry in the future.

CHAPTER 6

A Church Made Visible

Consider the possibility that most people in your community have never heard of your church. Don't know where it is. Don't know what it does. Wouldn't miss it if it weren't there.

You need to introduce yourself to these people. You need to find ways to get politely in their way. They cannot join you if you aren't visible and you aren't attractive to them. To begin this process, you need to take a good long look at how you are seen and how to improve your chances of being seen by more people in a favorable light.

Location, Location, Location

The process begins with a simple physical inventory. Do you have a building? If so, can people see it? If so, do most people see it while on foot—in which case they would have time to do a little reading as they walked by—or do they see it while driving in a car—in which case your name is probably all they could absorb.

If you've got a building, ask yourself when the greatest numbers of people are present in your neighborhood. We know of one parish that shares its parking lot with its county's government offices and courthouse. There are hundreds of workers and visitors within easy walking distance of the church, which is set in an area not known for its expansive array of lunchtime options. Yet the church is closed at that time of day. No noon prayer, noon music, noon book discussion. Nothing to invite a captive audience into the building.

We know of another parish that backs up onto the street where scores of parents wait in a carpool line every afternoon to pick up their children at school. All those parents—most of them mothers, the primary decision makers about church attendance in most American families—are sitting idle, and not a sign or banner in sight.

Some churches are blessed with excellent locations near the geographic centers of their communities, while others are obscurely situated and found primarily by those with a strong desire to find them. Fortunately, visibility, in the most literal sense, is not the only way in which a church can make its presence felt in a community. Borrow a page from the community organizer. Get out into your community and find out when people are home, where they congregate, how they spend their time in the neighborhood. Learn about the most popular coffee shops, restaurants, barbershops, gyms.

> Get out into your community and find out when people are home, where they congregate, how they spend their time in the neighborhood.

Find out how people spend their leisure time, whether your community holds particularly popular events like homecomings, picnics, or parades. On the weekends are the people in your neighborhood out on ball fields with their children, in bars drinking with their friends, or at movies with their dates? Are they running, biking, fishing, hunting, shopping? Pay attention to the institutions that bring people into your neighborhood. Does your church sit near an office complex, a community college, a specialty shop of some kind?

The demographics of your neighborhood matter immensely, so it is worth doing a little research to glean information that may not be visible to the naked eye. If you've got lots of families with school-age children, that dictates a different kind of outreach event than if you are speaking primarily to young single people who have moved into your vicinity to take their first job since college, or older couples whose children left home several years ago.

Economic factors are important as well. Do your neighbors have copious leisure time and not enough ways to use it? Are they stretched to the snapping point trying to maintain high standards at work and at home? Are they struggling just to get by?

> There is the circle of what your faith community has to offer and the circle of what your neighbors most need or want. Focus on the place where those two circles overlap.

Do people in your neighborhood live in single-family homes? Or do they live in apartments in which space might be tight, and another location in which to spend some time might be welcome?

If you are going to speak effectively to people, you need some sense of their hopes, their fears, and their needs. How can you help them achieve a goal, answer a question, heal a wound, provide support?

Think of effective visibility work as drawing a Venn diagram. There is the circle of what your faith community has to offer and the circle of what your neighbors most need or want. Focus on the place where those two circles overlap.

You can call attention to the things that your faith community has to offer its neighbors using the communications tools we discussed in previous chapters, and we will discuss ways to do that. But much of the work of making your church visible involves word of mouth, referrals, and engaging in the activities that put the name of your faith community on people's lips.

The focus of this book notwithstanding, most communication does not involve media of any sort. And when it comes to making an intensely personal decision such as attending a church, the recommendation of a friend carries considerable weight. It's worth knowing, then, who the influential people are in your community. Who has the broadest networks, both in person and online? What cliques, clusters, and interest groups might be mobilized to help you? Who are the most influential people in each?

In one community it might be useful to have the mayor on your side, in another the football coach, and in a third the unassuming couple with numerous children who due to the size of their family and the warmth of their welcome serve as second parents to half the children in the neighborhood.

No Steeple. Lots of People

We have learned a lot about making your church visible from the example of one church that did not have a building, and one congregation that, technically speaking, had not yet come into existence.

St. Alban's Church in Arlington, Texas, was among those that lost its property when the majority of the parish decided to join the man who was then the bishop of the Diocese of Fort Worth in leaving the Episcopal Church.[4] The people of St. Alban's moved their Sunday services into a playhouse, Theater Arlington. They celebrated the Eucharist on the stage, in front of the sets of whatever play was currently on offer.

Since the people of St. Alban's have no permanent place to call their home, they cannot leverage the visibility of their property or the usefulness of their facilities to attract newcomers to the church. Instead, they have no alternative but to be active and visible in their communities, working in partnership with

---

[4] Efforts to regain control of the property were underway but not yet concluded when this book went to press.

other organizations—showing the flag, so to speak, at parades and picnics, and being caught in the act of living out their faith. They have celebrated "Pentecost in the Park," adopted an Arlington public elementary school, developed a campus ministry at the University of Texas at Arlington, and, of course, sponsored outings to Theater Arlington. When we visited, the church without a church was larger than the average Episcopal congregation and welcomed visitors in as friendly but un-pushy a way as any congregation we've visited. And, yes, it's growing.

In Salem, Massachusetts, the Reverend Daniel Vélez Rivera and Deacon Ema Rosero-Nordalm built a Latino congregation at St. Peter's Episcopal Church where none had existed, but they did not hold services right away. In an interview we conducted for the Episcopal Church Foundation, Daniel told us about the birth of Iglesia Episcopal San Pedro.

> We spent a year canvassing the community, asking what were the holes in the community: secular and spiritual needs. We visited every stakeholder in the neighborhood, from restaurant owners to barbershop owners to people in the street. I volunteered at the department of youth services and VOCES (an immigration services agency). We didn't even hold a worship service for eight months.

What he and Ema learned was that the Spanish-speaking community in Salem was composed disproportionately of single mothers of different ages, many of whom had just arrived in the United States.

> It was clear that what was lacking was "How do you do things in this country? How do I deal with my children who are bicultural when I don't even speak English? How do I cope?" So we asked the question "Where is God in your need?" and what came out of many, many conversations was the idea to provide women with a group in which they could use the resources they already had—such as their faith—to help one another.

Daniel and Ema responded with a five-week intergenerational pilot program, *Abuelas, Madres y Más (Grandmothers, Mothers and More),* in which women shared their stories, their joys, and their struggles, and offered one another support. "We started with twelve women in the original group," Daniel says. "They were the first members of the parish. Once they became empowered, they wanted to be mentors for other women like themselves."

Now these women are the backbone of the parish. "They do the diaper ministry," says Daniel, who has since left Salem. "They do evening prayer. They preach. They are lay eucharistic visitors. It is not just sitting around in a circle talking about faith. . . . Now it is the bones of the church. More than the bones. It is the feet and the hands and the ears and the eyes of Christ in the community."

Your congregation probably has a building, and, in all likelihood, you are not starting your community from scratch. Still, the lessons that the folk at St. Alban's learned and the tactics that Daniel and Ema employed can be adapted by anyone.

Let's Talk About Faith

You may, however, have to get the people of your congregation past their fear of talking about their faith. Jim has a friend who is a Congregationalist minister in Maryland. She and a colleague were interested in helping people speak more easily about their faith to friends and neighbors. They assumed, as many educators do, that people would feel more comfortable talking about their faith if they had more information about it, and so they developed an eight-session course, a kind of Christianity 101 that hit all the high points of church history and the basics of theology.

When the course was over, the two ministers asked participants to evaluate it. Most people loved it. Many asked for additional instruction. One person suggested that they take each individual session and explore it more deeply in a single eight-session course devoted exclusively to that topic. The ministers were pleased at first, until they realized that rather than making people more comfortable in talking about their faith, they had made them less comfortable. Eight courses were not enough. At least one person wanted sixty-four!

This led Jim's friend and her colleague to a conceptual breakthrough. People were never going to feel that they "knew enough" about Christianity to explain their religion to others. If you wanted people to speak to other people about their faith, you had to put them on firmer ground. You had to focus the conversation on something in which they were experts: What was God doing in their lives? What was God doing in their community? How were they responding to God's activity? Their next course focused on demonstrating to people that they already "knew enough" to talk about God with their friends, and that sharing their feelings about what was happening in their lives was something that many friends would welcome.

There are a number of programs geared to initiating these kinds of conversations, including *Talking Faith* by Heather Kirk-Davidoff and Nancy Wood-Lyczak[5] (who were kind enough to tell us the story above).

Steps for Increasing Visibility

Making your congregation more visible in the community, giving people a better sense of who you are, what you believe in, and how you live out those beliefs, and figuring out how to invite people into a deeper relationship requires training from people with expertise in congregational and ministry development. But to shoulder the communications part of the load, we recommend a procedure like this one to begin.

1. Examine your faith community's messages. (See chapter 2.) Given the audiences you hope to reach, what are the best ways to articulate those messages? What are the

---

[5] Heather Kirk-Davidoff and Nancy Wood-Lyczak, *Talking Faith: An Eight-Part Study on Growing and Sharing Your Faith* (St. Louis, Mo.: Chalice Press, 2004).

kinds of services, events, programs, and practices that might appeal to these audiences?

2. Determine how best to disseminate these messages and publicize these events. (See chapters 3 and 4.) You've got various communications tools, but chances are you are speaking primarily to people who already know your faith community well. How can you catch other people's eyes?

3. Train clergy and lay members in rudimentary public and media relations techniques. (See chapter 5.) This can be done in a day-long seminar, possibly sponsored by a judicatory or a regional clergy association. The training should focus on writing media releases, taking advantage of free publicity opportunities, keeping a website on message, and responding to news events with statements and programming that will appeal to key audiences.

4. Explore materials that help people to get comfortable speaking about their faith. Once you have found a curriculum or format that suits your community, give it a try.

5. Compose a timeline of visibility-related activities to guide your efforts for twelve to eighteen months. You don't have to plan a dozen major events, just a couple to get you started.

Sample Visibility Report

We want to close this chapter by walking you through one of the "visibility reports" that Jim did for about two dozen parishes in the Episcopal Diocese of Washington in 2004. The audiences, opportunities and challenges that this parish encountered may not be similar to yours, but we think it is useful to see the kind of analysis and the sorts of tactics on which visibility work is based. As is common practice in Episcopal circles, a fictional parish created to serve as a notional example of a certain theory or situation will be referred to as St. Swithin's in the Swamp.

ST. SWITHIN'S IN THE SWAMP, VISIBILITY ANALYSIS

Description

The neighborhood surrounding St. Swithin's in the Swamp is being transformed by two important forces: an influx of immigrants—most of them Latino—and the long hoped for revival of downtown Swamp as a center of commerce and entertainment. St. Swithin's also has a significant but heretofore overlooked community on its doorstep: the students and faculty of Nearby Community College, a two-year commuter school that now caters primarily to immigrants.

The area is relatively well served by mass transit. Commercial areas and a Metro stop are nearby, but not necessarily within walking distance. There are several public parks in the area where people—especially young people—gather in warm weather. There is also a local youth theater company with which the parish already has a relationship. The parish property opens onto a busy thoroughfare on the south, and a public elementary school on the north side.

The nearby Swamp entertainment district includes a plaza built around a fountain and surrounded by restaurants that are frequented at lunch time by employees of Major Corporation, which has its world headquarters a few blocks away, and other office workers and, in the evenings, by local residents and moviegoers. The district includes a newly opened twenty-screen commercial theater, the Swamp Theater, which is home to the Swamp Cinema Institute and a new outpost of Brackish Water Theater Company. There is also an older business district along Bullfrog Avenue about a third of a mile west of the church, and a Latino-oriented business district nearby.

Two major north-south thoroughfares—Bullfrog Avenue and Nonpoisonous Snake Road—pass not far from the church. The community is served by the mammoth

Swamp High School. Swamp Youth Soccer and Swamp Babe Ruth are popular children's sports leagues.

The neighborhoods in which most parishioners live are served by two community newspapers as well as the Swamp County weekly edition of *The Washington Post*.

Discussion and Recommendations

St. Swithin's has a plethora of opportunities to engage people in public places: in the plaza of the new entertainment district, at ball fields, school events, and in the several business districts in the surrounding neighborhood. Many of these opportunities require more in the way of energy than of money. Perhaps the parish will consider some of the following suggestions:

a) Make use of the parish hall to host events for specific neighborhood groups: residents of the apartment complex next door, Latino sports fans who lack cable TV, students of Swamp College. (Invitation via leafletting in business district and condo and apartment complexes in the neighborhood in addition to yard signs at church.)

b) Explore having hospitality tables in local parks, especially at youth sports events and during peak usage hours such as early evening and on weekends.

c) Sponsor recreational events for the community in the field behind Swamp Elementary, followed by refreshments in the parish hall.

d) Distribute seasonally themed yard signs in the spring to residents who live near the church or in Swamp Highlands, a community that is home to many members of St. Swithin's.

e) Contact local merchants to explore 1) placing window signs, 2) leaving literature, 3) placing a St. Swithin's-sponsored "change for charity" receptacle beside their cash register (proceeds to Swamp County Community Ministries, or the like).

f) Contact merchants and locally-based companies to explore commercial sponsorship of community events initiated by St. Swithin's, and perhaps held on its grounds—anything from a two-hour moon-bounce rental to a bike safety clinic, to a pupusa-making cook off.

g) Continue its visibility at community events such as the Swamp County Music Jam. Consider involvement in other festivals and parades.

h) Look into potentially low-cost, well-targeted advertising in venues such as playbills of local theaters and playbills and sports programs at Swamp High School.

i) Explore ways to be visible in the entertainment district. These might include having the young parish chamber musicians offer a brief free concert on the plaza; holding post-play or post-movie receptions or "film talks" in the parish hall; partnering with Swamp Theater for a faith- or spirituality-themed film festival; hosting readings and coffeehouses aimed at young singles and couples. Or, establish a Parents Night Out service which, on one weekend night per month, would offer babysitting in the parish hall for parents who want to get away for a few hours to have dinner or take in a movie. This event might be coordinated with local restaurants and theaters. These establishments might be willing to help defray the cost or include St. Swithin's and its babysitting program in their advertising.

St. Swithin's Physical Plant

1) The Algae Avenue entrance presents significant challenges to visibility. The church and its permanent sign sit back from the street, and the sign in particular is hard to see and impossible to read from a passing car. In addition,

the flower shop next door obscures visibility from vehicles traveling west on Algae Avenue. *Recommendation:* Consider large, bright, ground-anchored banners angled toward traffic.

2) The East Ooze Avenue entrance has two drawbacks. A) The building, seen from this angle, looks more like a school than a church, and a fairly drab one at that. *Recommendation:* building-hung banners and plantings near the foundation would help brighten it up. B) The un-landscaped bank that leads to the parish house is untidy, obscures visibility of the grounds and is difficult to scale—thus acting as a barrier. The tall trees further obscure visibility. *Recommendation:* consider landscaping and planting on the bank, cutting a flight of broad, inviting stairs into it, and pruning off the lower branches of the evergreens.

3) The East Ooze entrance is seen daily by scores of parents whose children attend Swamp Elementary. *Recommendation:* A yard sign or large well-anchored white board with regularly changing messages and invitations would catch this audience's eye.

Outlets and Opportunities

Media (ads, releases, coverage requests)
• The local high school newspaper, two community-based newspapers, two community-targeted newspapers owned by *The Washington Post,* two Spanish-language newspapers.

Advertising
• Ads could be placed at all of the above outlets, plus in the programs of the local high school's play, musical, and sporting events and in the programs of the local theater companies and film festivals; fence signs at the local ballpark; bus ads on local routes; subway ads in nearest station;

onscreen ads in movie theaters. (Most parishes will need to participate in a cooperative buy with other parishes, or seek diocesan assistance.)

Public spaces (non-commercial)
• Community news boards at the local community college, local parades and music festivals.

Commercial targets
• All area merchants, with an emphasis on coffee shops and others places where people gather.

Neighborhood opportunities
• Inviting residents of condo complexes and apartment buildings to a special reception for members of their building or residents of their street at the church. Yard signs.

Outreach activities
• Invite local Latino community to Soccer Night (need big screen TV and cable);
• Cold drinks (with literature) youth sporting events;
• Hospitality tables (snacks, drinks) in local parks;
• Organized recreation on elementary school field: kickball, Frisbee golf, badminton, etc.;
• Coffee House nights (entertainment? readings?) for students at local community college;
• Single-parent dating night;
• Feed people's parking meters in the local business district and slip a notice telling them what you've done beneath their windshield wiper.

––––––––––––

Obviously no parish can undertake all of these activities. But most parishes can adopt some to their particular circumstances. If mainline churches are going to have an impact in their communities, they will have to learn the art of inviting their neighbors to "Come and see" in a language that those neighbors can understand.

CHAPTER 7

Speaking Faithfully in a Crisis

The other chapters in this book are about getting people's attention so you can tell them about the power of God's work in your faith community. This chapter, however, is about what to do when you already have people's attention, but it is not for the reasons you would like.

Whether you're in a crisis because of natural disaster, human failure, or both, the situation requires responsive, comprehensive communications. Some crisis communications situations are the church's fault and some aren't, but nearly all give us a

> If you can communicate gracefully and faithfully in a crisis, it will say more about your ministry than postcards, websites, and banners ever could.

chance to demonstrate that the church is true to its values even—especially—when things go badly wrong. If you can communicate gracefully and faithfully in a crisis, it will say more about your ministry than postcards, websites, and banners ever could.

Plan for It

Every organization should have a comprehensive crisis plan, and communications should be an integral part of it. Many church judicatories have sample crisis plans for members to use, and if your organization is without a crisis plan, developing one should be a high priority. Writing the entire crisis plan is beyond the scope of this book, but here are some items to consider when developing its communications elements:

• The planned crisis communications chain of command should be clear, but make sure that your plan involves more than one leader in case the designated decision-maker or spokesperson is injured or dead, or is the person whose behavior has caused the crisis.

• If you are in a congregation or organization without a communications person, identify a trustworthy volunteer or consultant to handle this role for the duration of the crisis. Plan for this ahead of time and make sure the person you've chosen knows he or she is part of your plan and will be on call in the event of a crisis.

• Make sure that your organization is signed up with your community's emergency alert system. Be clear ahead of time about who will issue notices about closings or other emergency protocol, but be sure that more than one person can access the system if needed. (If you need help with this, find a colleague in a climate where it snows. They'll know all about this kind of system.)

• Make sure at least two people can update your website from a remote computer if necessary.

• Keep printed and stored offsite in a safe, dry place a contact list of your organization's leaders including home addresses, cell phone numbers, and home phone numbers. If offices are destroyed and phone lines go down in a disaster, you may need to find people by going to their houses. If you can, also store this information in the cloud.

✒ Have your media list, including cell phone numbers and emails, printed and stored offsite in a safe, dry place where you can get it if your office is inaccessible due to natural disaster. Include leaders and communications officers of important partner organizations. If you can, also store this information in the cloud.

✒ Keep usernames and passwords stored offsite in a safe, dry place and in the cloud. Make sure than more than one trustworthy person knows how to access them.

✒ Keep sufficient biographical information on all of your organization's leaders so that you can write obituaries if needed or provide factual information to media producing stories about a leader's murder, suicide, death, or indictment.

✒ Your organization should practice its overall crisis plan regularly and people with communications responsibility should participate actively. How quickly can you access usernames, passwords, media lists, and other information? Are they up to date? Do you have the information you need on file to communicate accurately and comprehensively?

Most of this chapter is devoted to dealing with the media in a crisis. When your crisis involves misunderstanding, conflict, impropriety, or outright crimes, you will need to devote a lot of time to making sure people get accurate information in a timely and sensitive fashion.

Crisis Media Relations

Often the best opportunity to speak faithfully in the media comes when something goes badly wrong and it's the church's fault. You have the media's attention, and you have the opportunity to demonstrate that the church is willing to tell the truth, confess its sins and shortcomings when necessary, and seek forgiveness and reconciliation.

Unfortunately, this is exactly when the temptation to avoid the media is greatest and when the instinct to protect reputations, endowments, and power structures is strongest. But even if hiding from bad news is possible, it is generally not a good idea. Churches have a particular responsibility to speak the truth in a timely and transparent way even when it's uncomfortable. And when we don't, the culture of secrecy that takes hold ultimately deforms our ability to follow the way of the gospel.

As in all of the other case studies we have shared, when confronted with a crisis, you first have to determine the outcome you hope for and the audiences you need to reach to achieve that outcome. We are firm believers that the outcomes that Christian organizations should want to achieve when confronted with crises must be grounded in honesty, humility, and, where necessary, repentance.

> Christian organizations should want to achieve outcomes grounded in honesty, humility, and, where necessary, repentance.

A strategy that seeks first to guard the privacy or secrecy of the institutional church, the reputations of leaders who have done wrong, or the feelings of their families, or that seeks to provide cover for legal tactics that shirk responsibility for paying the cost of misdeeds or errors, will backfire—probably in the short-term, and certainly in the long-term—through either public relations catastrophe or institutional corrosion. In a crisis, your organization is under the lens of the wider church and the community, and you have the opportunity either to demonstrate your Christian values or to violate them. If we behave like Jesus when nothing is at stake and a legal team when everything is at stake, very little else we do in the way of evangelism will matter.

There are four simple rules for handling media in a crisis. They are easy to understand, but can be quite difficult to apply:

1. Tell your own bad news.

2. Tell it quickly.

3. Tell it all.

4. Don't let the lawyers run the show.

1. Tell your own bad news.

The reasons for this rule are probably self-explanatory. If something difficult and media-worthy is happening—often related to sex or money, and sometimes both—you want to make sure that the story that gets told to the world through the media is accurate and includes any mitigating circumstances or steps that the church is taking to set things right.

How do you know if your bad news rises to the level of requiring media disclosure? There are a few questions to ask yourself:

• Does the news involve a leader elected or chosen by church members? Would the members' ability to provide oversight be compromised if they did not know the news?

• Do people at church and in the wider community need to know about the news so that they can safeguard children, assets, or anything else from someone they might otherwise have trusted?

• Does the church need to ask forgiveness and make amends for past sins of commission or omission?

• Is the news going to get released by someone else if you don't do it?

❧ Is the news going to become public unless you take active steps to cover it up?

If the answer to any of these questions is yes, then you've got news to tell.

Once you have determined that you need to disclose bad news, you will want to develop a carefully choreographed plan. To start, identify your internal audiences and develop a plan to tell them first. Your people—whether they are congregation members, clergy, advocates, or community leaders—will take things better if they hear from you before they read it in the newspaper or hear it on the radio.

For both clarity and to keep community anxiety at a minimum, in a crisis it's important to establish one authoritative spokesperson and communications source for disseminating information about the crisis. It can be helpful to cultivate surrogates and allies who can carry your messages, but you must release your own news.

2. Tell it quickly.

The news industry operates 24/7, and waiting any time at all before addressing reporters' questions could cause you to miss the news cycle and get caught having to play defense against a story that uses someone else's version of the events as its foundation. What's more, news stories for which church leaders were "unavailable for comment" can stoke mistrust of religious authority in ways that make readers, and sometimes reporters, unwilling to hear much of anything else that the church needs to say.

When you have bad news that either must go public for transparency's sake or will go public because of media interest, tell your news to the media as soon as you have told it to your internal constituency. Make every effort to disclose the facts before anyone else with information about the bad news goes public. If you are facing a lawsuit, have discovered an abuser, are terminating a clergy member or employee for boundary violations or disciplinary reasons, or announcing other bad news, a media release is generally the best way to go. It ensures that all media will get the same version of the story. You may choose to combine a release with a one-on-one interview if a reporter has exclusive information on a story, or if you have a longstanding relationship with the reporter.

Bad news seems seldom to come to light between 9 a.m. and 5 p.m., Monday through Friday, and so when a crisis is happening, both the person handling communications and the principal spokespeople need to be available around the clock. We are as much in favor of sabbath time, drawing boundaries with work, and unplugging to seek balance as the next Christian, but during a crisis, those bets are off.

3. Tell it all.

Here is a crisis communications person's worst nightmare: A reporter who has been following a story contacts you because she has a new piece of information or evidence—a cancelled check, a victim's statement, a reliable witness—and you have never heard about what she says she's got. You ask the reporter when she needs a response and then call the leader in charge of the crisis. You relay the reporter's information and are met with a long, uncomfortable silence. You feel a pit in your stomach as you realize that what the reporter has told you is true, that your leaders knew about it, and that they did not tell you.

When you are disclosing a crisis, do not leave out important information, even if you think you might be able to get away with it. It's not honest, and if a reporter catches you doing it, you'll deserve a story that questions your organization's credibility. You will also have ruined your relationship with that reporter.

Another element in crisis communications is the pastoral care of the community affected by the crisis. Withholding information that will either reassure that community or allow them to come to terms with the full scope of what has happened constitutes not only poor communications but poor pastoral care.

This rule doesn't mean that you need to disclose every sordid detail of a scandal or include tangential information that might hurt innocent people. However, the institutional church's tendency is too often to keep things quiet or tell half-truths in order to avoid embarrassing or discrediting leaders who knew about wrongdoing, but did nothing. If you have to disclose offenses on the part of a church leader, and you know that other church leaders looked the other way or actively colluded, then you have a moral obligation to say so. You will also be protecting your organization against compounding the original crisis with a second crisis of confidence, and you will be sparing the organization the distortions that occur in relationships between people who know the secret and people who don't.

Protecting the church or its leaders—or even the memory of dead leaders—with silence or half-truths, consigns the church to what William Stringfellow called the "ethic of survival," which values the reputation of the institution above the values of the gospel or the needs of victims and survivors. One need only look at the Roman Catholic Church's handling of its pedophilia scandal to see the way in which telling lies to protect church leaders can cascade into a crisis of credibility and shame.

4. Don't let the lawyers run the show.

We have been privileged to work with several church lawyers who are the exceptions that prove this rule. These are the lawyers who help the church operate responsibly in the legal world and use the tools of the law to do justice and seek mercy. When a crisis communications team is fortunate enough to include one of these lawyers, it's possible to turn a crisis into a profound opportunity for evangelism by demonstrating that the church can live according to its own precepts, even when things are very difficult.

Ideally, a crisis should be managed by the canonical authority, the church attorney, and the communications person. In
the best situations—and there are many across the church—
the church lawyer will believe in the communications principles
outlined above and the communications person will understand
the legal strategy well enough to be respectful of it.

Old institutional habits die hard, however, and too often,
church lawyers act not as advocates of justice but as protectors
of authority and money. When
faced with the threatened choice
between bankrupting the institution and losing credibility as a
Christian organization, leaders
too often assume that is it easier
to recover from the latter than
the former. Moreover, even
lawyers familiar with the polity
of churches in which laypeople
exercise significant authority

> The best, most ethical
> communications strategy
> is sometimes in conflict
> with the legal strategy
> recommended
> by attorneys.

sometimes proceed in ways that deprive the members of the
information they need if they are to hold their leaders accountable.

Communications in these situations can be very difficult, because the best, most ethical communications strategy is sometimes in conflict with the legal strategy recommended by
attorneys who want to safeguard monetary assets, and the reputations of those in authority. Not surprisingly, in these situations, decision-makers may be reluctant to keep the
communications person in the loop and to take that person's
advice. Whether you are a clergyperson, a communications person, or an elected leader, if you find yourself in this kind of situation, you may have difficult decisions to make about your
own obligations and responsibilities as a professional person
and a Christian.

Contentious Communications

At the outset of any crisis situation, you need to define your audiences clearly and figure out if any of them are likely to organize against you. When you have organized opposition, you can try to anticipate it, and you can gauge whether or not its effect will be long-lasting or dissipate by the end of the news cycle, but you probably cannot control it or persuade it to see things your way—at least not through public communications. However, sometimes in crisis situations leaders can meet for private conversations that will have a positive effect on public rhetoric.

In a crisis with organized opposition, you can also try to be clear about which audiences you can reach with your information and messages, and which are set against you in ways that in all likelihood cannot be overcome. Your communications efforts and energy should be targeted to audiences who:

➤ Support you and need communications that will reinforce and justify their support and provide them with messages they can use in their own conversations and social media posts about the issue.

➤ May have sympathy for your opposition but who are open to a reasonable discussion. We often use the shorthand "movable middle" to refer to this audience.

➤ Have little or no previous familiarity with the issues at hand, but who are made aware of the situation because of heightened media attention. This audience is often much less concerned with the details of the situation than with how the church leaders they read, hear, and see in the media comport themselves.

Part of the job in this kind of crisis is keeping your leaders and spokespeople from responding to overwrought provocation in kind. This will only result in an escalated emotional battle that any reporter would find entertaining. You have to stay calm enough to judge whether or not your opponents' attack against you is newsworthy in its own right, or whether your response will be the thing that makes the negative situation newsworthy by creating a debate or a controversy. In the first instance, you are best served by making a response; in the second, you are best served by remaining quiet.

It is tempting to pour communications resources into arguing point-by-point with audiences who do not wish you well and whom you can't win over, but it is not a wise use of your energy. Instead, put your energy into proactive communications that will keep your opposition from gaining momentum and demonstrate to the world that you are trustworthy, even when under attack.

> Put your energy into proactive communications that demonstrate to the world that you are trustworthy.

In all contentious communications situations, it's important to remember that the media and the general public hold the church to higher standards than they hold themselves. This can be frustrating and seem unfair when you are being attacked, but it has been our repeated experience that aggressive or confrontational rhetoric from church leaders elicits a chorus of commentary about how the church is a fallen secular institution unworthy of trust or support. Toning down statements and talking points nearly always serves best in the long run, even if it feels in the moment as though you are taking it on the chin—or turning the other cheek.

Case Studies

We hope that you will never have to learn crisis communications on the job. But if you do, here are three case studies of different kinds of crises that can help you think about your own crisis communications plan so you are ready when the time comes:

Case 1. Building Bridges to Solve a Crisis:
The Diocese of Northern Michigan

Sometimes you find yourself in a crisis just because people mis-understand who you are and what you are doing. And if this misunderstanding takes hold, simply setting the record straight in a factual statement is not enough. These circumstances pre-sented a particular problem for the Episcopal Diocese of North-ern Michigan in 2008 and 2009.

The diocese's beloved bishop had been killed in a car acci-dent. After an unconventional process, the diocese chose a much beloved priest of the diocese as his successor. But the priest had theological and liturgical practices that were per-ceived to be out of the mainstream, and the wider church re-fused to consent to the election. The small, geographically isolated diocese found itself without a bishop and feeling as though its fellow Episcopalians had failed to appreciate the dio-cese's commitment to the church, the remote context in which it ministered, and the real hardship of managing for so long without a leader.

In this situation, it was essential to communicate each stage of the new search process to the people of the diocese and the leaders of the wider church much more completely and fre-quently than is usually the case. The standing committee and search committee committed to providing articles for the dioce-san newspaper and website and sending press releases to the church media explaining the new search process in ways that emphasized the diocese's commonality with the rest of the Episcopal Church.

At the same time, it was clear that the wider church needed to understand the ministry of the Diocese of Northern Michigan first-hand. The search committee responded by asking a well-respected retired bishop from another diocese to be the con-sultant to their search process and by inviting a number of leaders from the wider church to be guests at their diocesan convention.

These visits helped assure the people of the diocese that they mattered to the wider church, but more importantly, they established a cohort of church leaders who knew the leaders of the Diocese of Northern Michigan, and who understood more about the context of their ministry. In turn, the visits helped the diocesan leaders to understand the concerns of detractors in the wider church.

During the search process, the leaders of the diocese monitored the blogosphere, addressed misinformation quickly and clearly, and developed communications materials to address any aspects of the search that involved practices not familiar to people in other parts of the church.

The electing convention was reported upon as it happened via social media. News releases were in circulation within minutes of the election. The immediacy of this reporting reinforced the diocese's commitment to transparency and its commitment to the election practices favored by the wider church.

The story has a very happy ending: a long-time priest of the diocese was elected as the new bishop and easily received the consent of the wider church. People's interest in the situation proved to be an excellent hook to introduce him through the church and secular media.

Case 2. When Self-Interest Takes Over: Closing a Church School

This situation was common enough: A church that had supported a parish elementary school for more than fifteen years found that declining enrollment and rising costs had made the ministry unsustainable. The decision to close the elementary school was made easier by the fact that the great majority of its students were not members of the parish. Moreover, although they were receiving an excellent education subsidized by the parish, they were not living in particular economic need.

It is easy for people who are trying to keep a school open to represent themselves as the ones with children's best interests at heart. Having the conversation on those terms is a losing proposition, so the rector and the vestry worked to shift the conversation to focus on their primary concern: the best use of the church's resources for ministry. No one disputed that the school was providing a quality education for middle-class children whose parents preferred not to use the public schools. But it was clearly costing the parish money that might have been devoted to those in greater need. This way of framing the situation did not impress the parents of school children, but it did help to persuade the congregation and the media that there was a strong ethical case for closing the school. And these were the two audiences that mattered most in setting the tone for the way that the proposed closing was regarded in the wider community.

Once the church's core message was defined, parish leaders needed talking points and other documents to maintain calm conversations with increasingly emotional parents and teachers, prevent anxiety from spreading to the congregation and community, and resist the very human urge to argue against every attack that was made against them. While the communications team worked to deescalate the rhetoric and monitor online forums and social media where misinformation was rampant, the rector and leaders negotiated with a committee of parents who found a new home for the school under the auspices of a nearby church.

Case 3. Doing the Right Thing: *The Diocese of Northwestern Pennsylvania*

Among the most challenging crises a church can face is the sexual abuse of children by a church leader. In this situation, as the long and sordid history of the Roman Catholic sexual abuse crisis has made clear, the moral credibility of the institution is under threat. The church is also exposed to significant financial liability, and the faith and feelings of church members can be shaken because in many instances the abuser was someone whom they trusted, and the victims are their own children, the children of friends, or the children of their congregation.

In cases like these, communications people find themselves working in concert both with church leaders and with lawyers whose opinions range across the spectrum described earlier in this chapter. The approach can be further complicated in situations in which the abuse occurred in the past and has only now come to light. Because societal attitudes about sexual abuse and misconduct have changed so dramatically in the last twenty-five years, those who discover an old case of abuse and want to report it immediately sometimes face opposition from those who knew about the abuse, worked with the abuser, and thought that it was best to keep quiet at the time. Communicators must also reconcile the need to inform members of the community with the moral obligation to protect the identity and dignity of the victims and survivors of the abuse and their families.

In short, handling sexual abuse crises well requires a solid plan, a unified team, and a leader with the moral courage to set an honest, ethical course. In the summer of 2010, just this kind of leader—Bishop Sean Rowe of Northwestern Pennsylvania, whose offices are in Erie—received information about four women who had made credible allegations that they were sexually abused during childhood by his predecessor-once-removed.

From the outset, the bishop committed himself to telling the truth, calling for additional victims to come forward, and seeking forgiveness and reconciliation for acts that had been committed decades before by his now-dead predecessor. In addition, the diocesan chancellor, Jim Steadman, was a model of cooperation and collegiality who shared the bishop's desire to disclose the truth, a position he advocated in his conversations with other legal counsel involved in the situation.

Despite resistance from other quarters, Bishop Rowe and his team developed a carefully choreographed plan to inform the standing committee of the diocese of the situation and meet immediately afterward with the clergy of the diocese, all on a Saturday afternoon. The clergy received a pastoral letter from the bishop to be read and made available at all services the following morning. As soon as the Sunday morning services across the diocese were concluded, the letter was posted on the diocesan website and sent, with an accompanying press release, to the local media. Special care was taken to give a full background briefing to a reporter at the most influential newspaper in the diocese. In addition, the bishop worked hard to ensure that anyone with a personal connection to the late bishop heard the news from him before church on Sunday morning. The diocese also worked with communicators in dioceses where the predecessor in question had served as a priest before becoming bishop and where he had retired.

Bishop Rowe did media interviews for several days after the story broke to make sure that all of the community's questions were answered and that his voice would be heard in smaller communities that are not part of the Erie media market. After this initial disclosure of information, Bishop Rowe issued a statement outlining how the additional abuse complaints that had surfaced would be handled, and promised an update at the end of the summer. This allowed for a break in the media frenzy, and gave the bishop time to work pastorally with the victims, without making it appear as if the diocese were withholding information or refusing to speak on the matter. At the end of the summer, as promised, the bishop updated the diocese and the community about the situation.

It is a mark of success that, about eighteen months later, the *Erie Times-News* ran a highly positive story describing the diocese's strengthened sexual abuse prevention policy and new abuse reporting procedures. Out of the very worst kind of crisis, Bishop Rowe and the diocese have emerged as a model of how to handle communications in a crisis and how to prevent that kind of crisis from happening again.

Rebuking the Wind

It is easy to panic in a crisis. Remember the gospel story of the disciples who are in the boat with Jesus when a storm comes up (Mark 4:35–41)? They woke him from a nap and accused him of not caring if they perished with the ship. Jesus calmed the wind and the waves and scolded the disciples. "Why are you afraid? Have you still no faith?"

Not all crises are that easily solved. Sometimes the boat gets swamped and the winds don't abate. Sometimes the ship goes down. But no matter how bad the storm gets, we have, in the midst of it, an opportunity to speak faithfully when people are listening. To do so calmly and with humility is an act of evangelism that can heal, restore relationships, and even bring about resurrection. When you are faced with a crisis, imagine that you are in that little boat. You can choose to act like the disciples, or you can choose to act like Jesus. Choose Jesus.

> No matter how bad the storm gets, we have an opportunity to speak faithfully when people are listening.

Signs of Grace

Tell and Show

A few years ago, a friend of ours, the Reverend Bonnie A. Perry, was among those nominated to stand for election as bishop of the Episcopal Diocese of Minnesota. Bonnie is a lesbian, and at that particular moment her sexual orientation was a cause for even greater concern in the worldwide Anglican Communion, of which the Episcopal Church is a member, than it would be if she ran now.

The New York Times, which seldom cares who is nominated for bishop even within its own circulation area, was intrigued by the potentially disruptive nature of Bonnie's candidacy and called her up. In response to a question about why she was running for bishop at that delicate time and in the face of global disapproval, Bonnie said, in part, that she wanted to "bear witness to the Gospel of Jesus Christ that changes people's lives."

You could spend an entire career in church communications trying to get that sentence into *The New York Times* and not succeed. Few mainstream newspapers find themselves with reason to print such a straightforward profession of faith. But on August 2, 2009, a sentence that in its substance could have been lifted from the Acts of the Apostles appeared on Page A-13 of the most influential newspaper in the United States.

Our friend did not become the bishop of Minnesota, but her interview with the *Times* crystallized something for us. In a way, the church is always trying to tell the world that the gospel of Jesus Christ changes lives. If there is a single turnkey, off the rack, one-size-fits-all message for a Christian community, that may well be it. It isn't given to all of us to get that message into *The New York Times*. Indeed, it is hardly ever given to any of us. But we all have opportunities to proclaim the gospel through media relations, websites, social media, and other tools of mass communications in our own contexts.

> We all have opportunities to proclaim the gospel through media relations, websites, social media, and other tools of mass communications in our own contexts.

In these pages, we have offered our suggestions on how to formulate your statements or messages; how to figure out who you need to speak to; how to tell stories that illustrate that you mean what your messages say; what vehicles to use to tell those stories, and how best to use those vehicles. In the end, those of us who work in communications never outgrow the advice of thousands of high school composition teachers: back up your assertions with evidence.

Had *The New York Times* been writing a full blown profile of Bonnie, rather than just quoting her in a news story, its reporter would have learned that through her ministry, the gospel of Jesus Christ had, in fact, changed lives. It had revitalized a parish that was on the verge of closing, and inspired the creation of a successful social services agency that ministered to her city's poor. We mention this not to toot her horn, but to point out a pattern: audacious assertion supported by solid evidence. This is how we bring the timeless message of the gospel to life in our time, and in your place.

As we have worked on this book, Jim has remembered the definition of a sacrament that he was taught as a child. A sacrament, the old Baltimore Catechism said, is "an outward sign instituted by Christ to give grace." As a communicator in the church, you tell stories of the outward signs through which your community responds to God's grace. In doing so, you create another sign—be it a newsletter, a webpage, or a mainstream media placement—through which the news of God's grace is conveyed to your community, and perhaps to the wider world. In this way, communications mimics our worship: it is both word (proclamation) and sacrament (a potentially transformative manifestation of God's grace).

Sometimes these signs are small, and have no audience beyond your faith community. Other times despite your best efforts, they fail to receive the attention they deserve. (Jim still can't believe that he couldn't get anyone to cover the construction of a playground in an empty lot, built during a single day by a cast of dozens and used by the students at the tuition-free Bishop John T. Walker School for Boys in Washington, D. C.) At other times, though, through combinations of chance, preparation, relationships, and skill, the church speaks, and people pay attention.

Ashes, Ashes

In 2012, the Episcopal Diocese of Chicago asked us to help publicize "Ashes to Go," an exercise in liturgical evangelism in which priest and lay people take to street corners, parks, squares, campuses, bus stops, and train stations on Ash Wednesday to make the sign of the cross in ash on the foreheads of willing passersby, reminding them that they are mortal and in need of redemption. The effort was headed by the Reverend Emily Mellott and supported by Bishop Jeffrey Lee. In two previous years, the diocese had received some excellent local coverage of this event, as the media seemed intrigued by the notion that a sacred act could be performed in a secular space. And besides, the pictures of clergy and lay people in black cassocks and white surplices were rather diverting.

Emily was hoping to build the Ashes to Go network in her diocese, and also to make the various practitioners of Ashes to Go across the country aware of one another, so she had begun a website, asking her clergy colleagues to let her know if they were taking ashes into the streets so she could help publicize their activities. Emily's fast-developing network proved to be essential. It gave us the evidence we needed to pitch Ashes to Go to both the Chicago media (which had covered it in the past, thanks to the work of Canon David Skidmore, the former diocesan communications officer) and to the national media, which was largely unaware of it.

Two weeks before Ash Wednesday, we sent out the following release to religion writers across the country, in addition to different releases in Chicago and its suburbs.

EPISCOPAL CHURCHES TAKE ASH WEDNESDAY SERVICES INTO THE STREETS

Fast-growing "Ashes to Go" initiative "brings church out here to us"

CHICAGO, FEBRUARY 16—More than 40 Episcopal parishes in 11 states will take to the streets on Ash Wednesday, February 22, marking the beginning of the holy season of Lent by giving "Ashes to Go."

In Chicago, St. Louis, New York, San Francisco, Seattle, Baltimore, Newark, Erie, Austin and other cities and suburbs around the country, priests and lay people will visit train stations, subway stops, coffee shops, and street corners to mark the forehead of interested passers-by with the sign of the cross, and invite them to repent of their past wrongdoing and seek forgiveness and renewal.

"Ashes to Go is about bringing spirit, belief, and belonging out from behind church doors, and into the places where we go every day," says the Rev. Emily Mellott, rector of Calvary Episcopal Church, Lombard, Ill., who is organizing the initiative in the Diocese of Chicago, where more than 20 churches are expected to participate. "It's a simple event with deep meaning, drawing on centuries of tradition and worship to provide a contemporary moment of grace."

Mellott learned about Ashes to Go from the Rev. Teresa K. M. Danieley, of St. John's Episcopal Church, St. Louis, Mo., who began conducting a street corner service with the distribution of ashes in 2007.

"On the street corner, we encounter people who have been hurt by previous experiences with organized religion and who, through Ashes to Go, take a tentative step back towards attending Church," Danieley says.

The Rt. Rev. Jeff Lee, Bishop of Chicago, is an enthusiastic supporter of marking Ash Wednesday in the streets. "My most memorable experience last year was with a woman who told me that she had left the church years ago," he says. "She received the ashes and our prayers gratefully and then she looked up and with tears in her eyes, she said to me, 'I just can't believe you would bring the church out here to us.'"

The release included a link to Emily's Ashes to Go website and to an essay and photographs that the author Sara Miles of St. Gregory of Nyssa Episcopal Church in San Francisco had contributed to the Episcopal Café website the previous year.[6]

You can begin to see pieces of a puzzle come together here. To Emily's web- and emailed-based outreach, we added a press release, and then began promoting Ashes to Go on the diocese's e-newsletter, on its Facebook page, and in its Twitter stream. We culled photographs by Canon Skidmore and others from the diocesan archives and pushed some out through the diocesan communications channels, but held on to others in case the media asked for previously unpublished material.

---

[6] Sara Miles, "Ash Wednesday in the Streets," Episcopal Café, March 9, 2011; http://www.episcopalcafe.com/daily/church_year/ash_wednesday_in_the_streets_1.php. Used by permission.

The effort didn't take off right away, though we were delighted to get a fairly quick response from Religion News Service, which has a wider reach in the Internet age than it did when it depended on newspapers to pick up its stuff. A few suburban Chicago papers were in touch, but with just a few days to go we weren't sure we would even replicate the success that Canon Skidmore had had the previous year. Then, just to be certain that she had received our original release, we sent another one to Cathy Grossman, the religion writer and blogger at *USA Today*. As it happens, she had been out of town when the first one arrived, and it was lost in an overflowing inbox. She got to work on the story almost immediately. She had something online that afternoon, and something in the paper the following morning.

Suddenly, it seemed that everyone was fascinated by Ashes to Go. The *CBS Morning News* featured *USA Today*'s coverage during its broadcast. *The New York Times* published four photographs of priests distributing ashes in the streets, and three of them were Episcopalians. The online edition of Newark's *Star-Ledger* published a video of Episcopal Bishop Mark Beckwith distributing ashes to commuters at a train station. Our colleague Neva Rae Fox at the Episcopal Church Center informed us that more than 250 news outlets covered Ashes to Go in some way, shape or form. Most of these were outlets we hadn't even been in touch with, evidence that—perhaps because of the *USA Today* and *CBS Morning News* stories—the Ashes to Go story was spreading on its own in the way of a joke, or a Facebook meme.

> What turns publicity into something akin to evangelism? The clearly sacramental nature of the act, coupled with the willingness of participating clergy and congregations to move out of their space and into the space of those they were trying to reach.

It is fair—it is always fair—when evaluating the importance of media coverage to ask oneself, so what? What turns publicity into something akin to evangelism? In this instance, we believe, it was the clearly sacramental nature of the act of giving ashes, coupled with the willingness of participating clergy and congregations to move out of their space and into the space of those they were trying to reach.

Amy Frykholm wrote movingly of what the ashes initiative meant to her in a *Christian Century* blog:

> I am currently a homeless Christian, a wanderer without a congregation. The reasons for my homelessness are, like most homelessness, complex. Since I have no readily available religious community, I have been worrying endlessly over where and how to receive ashes this coming Wednesday. Every option seems fraught with difficulties and problems. Ashes to Go speaks to me with an innate appeal....
>
> The idea is to bring the church, with its rites and symbols, to the people—not to force anything on them, but because forgiveness, repentance, introspection, a moment of connection and quiet are needed everywhere. Bishop Jeff Lee, of the diocese of Chicago, recalls a woman, who, upon receiving ashes from him said that she never imagined that "the church would come out here to us."
>
> Writing about Ashes to Go last year, Sara Miles tells of her fellow ash dispenser, Deb, being transfixed by the way that liturgy inserts timelessness in a place where people are constantly rushing. Miles writes: "'It's so intense,' she told me. 'Whenever your fingers touch the forehead, it's like time stops, over and over and over.'"
>
> I will absolutely place myself in these ash dispensers' path tomorrow, a hungry supplicant. And I will probably say "thank you" instead of "amen" after a kind stranger tells me that I am dust and to dust I will return.[7]

---

[7] Amy Frykholm, "Ashes for Wanderers," *Century Blogs,* February 21, 2012; http://www.christiancentury.org/blogs/archive/2012-02/ashes-wanderers.

As we mentioned earlier, Episcopalians constitute less than one percent of the United States' population, but through Ashes to Go the clergy and people of our church made our faith known to much of the country on the first day of Lent. We have recounted this story not (solely) because it speaks to the importance of a well-integrated communications plan or a timely pitch to the mainstream media. It also illustrates the kind of initiatives that we believe are important to the future of the church, and the ways in which two sometimes conflicting visions of the Christian future—the church as institution and the church as movement—actually nourish one another.

Speaking to a New World

Much of what we have discussed in these pages falls loosely under the heading of organizational communications. The church bears some similarities to a well-established nonprofit, cause-oriented organization. Outfits of that sort need well-honed messages that spring from their long-established identities. They need ways to reach members, ways to raise money, and they have to know how to keep their issues in the public eye in an ongoing way. That description fits the church, but it can't be our entire wardrobe.

Let us share some facts. People's attachments to organized religion today are exceedingly loose. According to a 2008 Pew Forum survey, 44 percent of American adults have changed religious affiliation at least once in their lives. People have lost faith in institutions of all kinds, and are seeking answers to life's most profound questions wherever they may find them. In addition, the rapid evolution of social media has undermined traditional hierarchies, and that includes spiritual hierarchies. When they comment on your

> The rapid evolution of social media has undermined traditional hierarchies, and that includes spiritual hierarchies.

Facebook status, your priest or bishop looks little different to the rest of your friends than your old college roommate or your running buddy. In the comments on a blog, the words of an eminent theologian are weighed on the same scale as the ones made by a guy who signs himself Dragonslayer643.

The church cannot assume it enjoys the institutional privileges it once did. It cannot assume that most of the world thinks well of us, or cares much about what we do. We have to work harder, be more inventive and more entrepreneurial. At the same time, we profess an ancient faith. And while God is still speaking, as the great Congregationalist slogan has it, we can't behave as though everything is up for grabs at every minute.

The Ashes to Go initiative depended on priests who were willing to step outside the mainstream of current liturgical practice. It required bishops who would support them. Perhaps more than any other single factor, it required someone willing to make the many scattered communities involved in this endeavor aware of one another. Without that awareness, there could be no national media release, just a lot of local news items that may or may not have been successful in the absence of attention from some of the country's agenda-setting newspaper and television programs. The church *is* an institution, and many denominations are hierarchical institutions at that. But that means that the church has institutional resources that can be deployed to support activities that function more like movements or campaigns.

It isn't entirely clear that those who lead the church as an institution can give those who lead the church as movement the freedom and support they need to help renew Christianity, or that those who see the church as a movement can build on momentary successes to gather followers rather than consumers of distinctive experiences. But communications people in the church must be able to serve whichever church is leading the way at the moment, and to facilitate the interplay between the two.

Seeding the Clouds

It is both the good news and the bad news of church communications that the institutions whose stories we tell and the tools that we use to tell those stories are evolving faster than at any point since Gutenberg helped kick-start the Reformation. You have to be willing to acquire new skills, and, what is harder, you have to be willing to relinquish old identities. Few of us have the luxury to specialize. When we do, our organizations tend to suffer. We have seen many good church journalists who wanted to continue to devote all of their time to being church journalists being forced out of their jobs. We have also seen church leaders hire people with primarily technical skills to lead communications efforts that require at least some facility in putting across a message, telling a story, or striking a mood.

Helping to publicize Ashes to Go was among the most satisfying experiences that we have had in church communications. But on the first Sunday of Lent, the pews of the Episcopal Church were not suddenly full. Our much-discussed numerical decline has moderated recently, but it has not yet stopped. If you work in church communications, there is a temptation to take this decline personally, to assume that if you were just doing more, or doing better, that you personally could persuade the great uninterested or religiously alienated public to haul themselves out of bed and into a pew on what might be the only lightly scheduled day in their week. There is also a temptation on the part of budget makers to assume that if a particular communications initiative doesn't immediately produce more members, then it isn't working. (We are familiar with more than one parish that abandoned an evangelism effort after sending out a single postcard because it hadn't produced results.)

Evangelism through communications seldom works swiftly. We can't predict how a story will affect those who hear it. The impact of our work on a person's faith journey is beyond our control. We seed the clouds, but only God can make it rain.

What we can do is keep telling stories, keep making sacraments, keep inviting people to "come and see," keep making our communities appealing to those without and stimulating to those within. Since God is still speaking, we must keep translating, narrating, announcing. This is what we can do, and it is all we can do. In the end there is only one job: to speak faithfully.